GAME OVER!

Strategies for Redirecting Inmate Deception

Bill Elliott, Ph.D., and Vicki Verdeyen, Ed.D.

American Correctional Association
Lanham, Maryland

American Correctional Association Staff

Printed in the United States of America by Versa Press, Inc., East Peoria, Il.

Mission Statement:
The American Correctional Association provides a professional organization for all individuals and groups, both public and private, that share a common goal of improving the justice system.

For information on publications and videos available from ACA, contact our worldwide web home page at: http://www.aca.org

ISBN 1-56991-160-6 (pbk)

Library of Congress Cataloging-in-Publication Data

Elliott, Bill, 1951-
    Game over! : strategies for redirecting inmate deception / Bill Elliott and Vicki Verdeyen.
        p. cm.
    Includes bibliographical references and index.
    ISBN 1-56991-160-6 (pbk.)
    1. Correctional psychology. 2. Prisoners–Psychology. 3. Deception. 4. Manipulative behavior. 5. Prisoners–Counseling of. I. Title: Inmate deception. II. Verdeyen, Vicki.
    III. Title.
    HV9276 .E55 2002
    365'.6–dc21   2002027744

This publication may be ordered from:
American Correctional Association
4380 Forbes Boulevard
Lanham, Maryland 20706-4322
1-800-222-5646

Acknowledgments

This book is dedicated to the countless men and women who work in the criminal justice system and struggle each and every day to make a difference in the lives of individuals who are characterized by their propensity for deception, manipulation, and exploitation. The authors hope that the strategies contained in these pages offer at least some assistance in leveling the playing field for those who serve to protect all of us through their work with offenders.

The first author expresses his gratitude to Rhonda Peacock, psychology technician, and Dr. Christopher Nolan, staff psychologist, at the U.S. Penitentiary at Terre Haute, Indiana for manuscript typing and editorial reviews, respectively. A special thank you goes to Dr. Glen Walters, whose lifestyle theory of criminal conduct provided the theoretical framework for this book. Finally, Dr. Elliott extends his everlasting appreciation to his wife, Sandy, who has provided support and encouragement at every step of his personal and professional development.

The second author wishes to thank Alice Fins, managing editor, American Correctional Association, who "sparked" the idea to write this book. To my coauthor, Bill "Doc" Elliott, who certainly is one of the best in the corrections business, I extend my sincere appreciation for his professional partnership throughout the years, and especially in this venture. Most of all, I want to express my gratitude to my husband, Bob, who shares the same commitment to the field of corrections, for his constancy and devotion and also to our children, Meagan and Michael, for the delight and joy they bring us every day.

Bill Elliott
Vicki Verdeyen

CONTENTS

Foreword

One of the biggest challenges facing correctional staff is dealing with deception and manipulation from the inmate population. Despite being behind bars, inmates can find numerous opportunities to exploit situations for their own advantage. Whether for some kind of gain or just for fun, the manipulative games inmates play can cause serious disruptions in the orderly operation of an institution. Well-meaning employees can find themselves in compromising positions, and talented professionals can have their careers ruined by being unwittingly manipulated by sly inmates.

Game Over! Strategies for Redirecting Inmate Deception helps correctional staff and volunteers recognize and respond to these con games by delving into the nature of inmate deception and manipulation. Drs. Elliott and Verdeyen discuss the aspects inherent in prison life that encourage inmates to lie and deceive. In addition, they explain how manipulation as a way of life is a reflection of the exploitative view that inmates have of others. By understanding the purpose and the perceived benefits of deceptive behavior, and by recognizing the situations that are most likely to allow such behavior to occur, correctional employees are in a better position to spot a set up or con and respond appropriately without being deceived.

Learning to identify inmate deception does more than protect the employees. It also provides positive treatment for the inmates. When inmates get away with deceiving staff, they do not gain anything. They merely continue the unhealthy behavior patterns that got them in trouble in the first place. By detecting and stopping their con games, correctional staff show inmates honesty and integrity in action, modeling prosocial skills that the inmates would do well to emulate.

James A. Gondles, Jr., CAE
Executive Director
American Correctional Association

PART I:
Learning the Game

Chapter 1

Introduction to Con Games

Why Write This Book?

Criminal justice professionals have a critical need for training to learn effective strategies for dealing with offenders on a day-to-day basis. Sometimes training programs focus too heavily on managing emergency situations and institution disturbances at the cost of training staff on the equally important strategies of everyday interaction with offenders. There are many excellent resources for learning interpersonal communication skills and for learning interviewing and individual and group counseling skills. The authors wanted to write a book specifically to address the unique "mind games" that one encounters when working with a criminal population. We hope this book will serve as a self-training experience to help you understand and manage inmate manipulation and deception, or "con games."

A word about what is therapeutic for criminal populations

Most traditional and free-world therapies were developed for individuals who are depressed, anxious, and have low self-esteem. Criminal justice workers who were trained this way are at a distinct disadvantage when they begin to work with offenders who are characterized by their general lack of anxiety, carefree attitudes, and love of themselves (narcissism). The traditional therapeutic approaches can quickly lead staff into the psychological traps set by those who only desire to manipulate and deceive them. Criminals do experience depression and anxiety, and empathy and support are appropriate at those times. However, the critical treatment targets are the criminal attitudes and behavior patterns that perpetuate crime. When staff and correctional programs fail to establish treatment goals of reducing criminal beliefs and needs, recidivism remains high (Andrews, 1998).

Throughout this book, the authors will concentrate on settings limits, avoiding criminal manipulation, and targeting the criminal belief or attitude underlying the offender's behavior. That does not mean staff should not respond to offenders with sympathy and support when appropriate. It does mean that it is critical to gain an understanding of which response is appropriate at which time.

Why a book specifically on inmate manipulation and deception?

It is true that correctional professionals are not pure and completely honest 100 percent of the time. All of us have engaged in a "con" game or manipulated someone to get what we want. This is not a book about occasional manipulative behavior by prosocial individuals. It is also true that offenders are not dishonest and manipulative 100 percent of the time. But this is not a book about offender behavior that is real and sincere. What is needed by criminal justice workers is information about the enduring criminal thinking patterns and behaviors of offenders and how to counteract them.

We know that criminal justice professionals are selected for their jobs because they have lived honest, responsible, prosocial (as opposed to antisocial) lives. Typically, their families of origin are solid citizens, and in fact, many have parents, uncles, aunts, and spouses who are career correctional or law enforcement professionals. Although, surely, all of us have been the victim of a scam or have been manipulated or deceived by someone before we started working with offenders, almost none of us have been engaged with antisocial, criminally oriented individuals on a daily basis. Dealing with someone who may periodically engage in manipulation or deception is quite different from dealing with people who know no other way of interacting with the world, including you. The authors hope this book will help you understand what to expect and how to respond when communicating with antisocial individuals who attempt to manipulate and deceive.

A Brief History of the Concept of Con Games

In 1961, Eric Berne, M.D., developed "transactional analysis" to describe a theoretical approach to understanding ourselves and how we relate to others in our social interactions. According to Berne (1961), there are specific repetitive social maneuvers between individuals that are defensive and self-gratifying. Individuals who engage in "games" with others, as opposed to interacting in honest communication, are living out "scripts" instead of living healthy, authentic lives. In his book, *Games People Play*, Berne (1964) defined a "game" as a series of transactions between people that were superficially plausible but had hidden agendas. In fact, "games" are uniquely characterized by their ulterior quality and the presence of a payoff (Berne, 1964). There are games played by married couples, games played by the client with the therapist, and games played by criminals with those who represent law enforcement. Berne (1964) grouped this last group together as "underworld games." They are played by criminals who derive psychological satisfaction and sometimes tangible gains from the probation officers, correctional officers, and others who have unwittingly set themselves up to be victims of the games.

In 1981, Allen and Bosta published *Games Criminals Play: How You Can Profit by Knowing Them*. This book elaborated on the work of Berne (1961,1964) and helped new correctional workers understand the motives of criminals and their own vulnerabilities. Our book extends these previous works by incorporating information about the psychology of inmate deception and manipulation, the specific criminal thinking patterns that are represented by these behaviors, and a review of games favored by women offenders.

Everyone who works with criminals needs to learn how to:

- Recognize the "first" moves used to set up a "con game"
- Decide which criminal thinking strategy the offender is using
- Learn to use the best "counter move" to shut down the game and ensure a win-win for you and the offender

You will learn how to do all of these things in *Game Over! Strategies for Redirecting Inmate Deception*.

Winning the Game

In most recreational games, there is a clear opponent, and someone wins and someone loses. In playing con games, we want to ensure that everybody wins. There is an interesting paradox in con games that staff need to appreciate: the offender thinks he or she wins if the staff member is successfully tricked, when in reality, if the staff member is tricked, the offender does not have the opportunity to learn how to interact honestly, a skill that is needed to maintain freedom in the community. When we know the strategies of winning at criminal game playing, we can respond to the offender in a way that teaches the appropriate way of interacting with noncriminal people, a skill they will need to maintain their freedom.

The reason we are present in the lives of offenders is to provide the prosocial context in which they must learn to live if they truly want to be a part of a free society. Letting offenders get by with their games, knowingly or unknowingly, only serves to reinforce and perpetuate criminal thinking and behavior. Purposeful redirection of attempts at manipulation and deception can become a force for an offender changing into a social being characterized by honesty and integrity.

Chapter 2

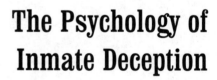

The Psychology of
Inmate Deception

Most observers of prison life have noted that deception and manipulation are central features of the inmate culture. Indeed, lying, conning, and game-playing are regarded by some as survival strategies in prison settings (Soderstrom, Castellano, and Figaro, 2001). Unsuspecting staff members are often the direct or indirect recipients of inmate deception and manipulation. The main purpose of this book is to help correctional employees accurately identify and effectively respond to such behavior before they find themselves in compromising situations.

However, it is first necessary to answer some fundamental questions concerning inmate deception and manipulation. For example, can these behaviors be classified or categorized in some way? In what psychological or social context does manipulation occur? Do staff members contribute to their own manipulation? What are the reasons or payoffs for such behavior? Finally, is manipulation related in any significant way to inmates' personality or lifestyle? We address these and related questions in this chapter.

Classification of Inmate Deception

Most forms of inmate deception can be classified as either lying by commission, lying by omission, dissimulation, or manipulation. All four of these "categories" are characterized by an attempt by one person (an inmate) to deceive another (a staff member). Further, there is considerable overlap between and among each "type" of deception.

Lying by commission. This type of lie is an untruth, told consciously with an intent to deceive, in which a piece of reality is deliberately distorted or invented (Gediman and Lieberman, 1996). Such lies are usually told about something of importance to mislead an audience. For example, if an inmate tells a chaplain that he needs to be idled from work due to a death in his family, when in fact there has been no such death, the inmate is lying by commission. The disadvantage of this kind of deception is that most outright lies are relatively easy to detect, given adequate time and initiative. For example, the chaplain, in collaboration with the inmate's counselor or case manager, would be wise to call a hospital, mortuary, or elsewhere to verify the inmate's report.

Lying by omission. This kind of lie, which is used much more frequently by inmates (Yochelson and Samenow, 1977), involves a conscious attempt to leave out certain information that would be important for an audience to know. In such instances, the deceiver tells some of the truth and, therefore, cannot be accused of "lying" in the strict sense of the word. For example, imagine that an inmate returns to his work assignment from a hospital appointment thirty minutes later than expected. When asked by his foreman for an explanation, the inmate replies that he ran into his counselor after the appointment and took advantage of the opportunity to discuss his visiting list. In this (all too common) scenario, the inmate did see his counselor and did mention a concern about his visitors. However, what he did not tell his boss was that the "discussion" with the counselor lasted only thirty seconds, that he (the inmate) went to the psychology department to sign up for the drug education program, that he strolled out to the prison factory to apply for a job, and that he stopped by his housing unit and smoked two cigarettes.

Dissimulation. Dissimulation is a general term that refers to deliberate distortion or misrepresentation of a psychological or a physical symptom (McCann, 1998). Dissimulation encompasses a variety of inaccurate defensive and inconsistent responses, all of which have a specific goal in mind. For example, inmates often present a nurse or physician's assistant with a request for a lower bunk pass due to a self-reported arm or leg problem, which allegedly interferes with climbing into or down from the top bunk. In many of these cases, the inmate's true concern is that of comfort and convenience. A similar scenario features an appeal to a psychologist to get a "mental health idle" due to unmanageable "stress" or "conflict" at the inmate's work assignment. In most cases, the inmate is actually seeking a day off from work to sleep, watch television, or engage in some prohibited activity.

Manipulation. Most of the examples of inmate deception described in this book exemplify "conning," prison slang for manipulation. Conning involves getting someone (staff) to do what the manipulator (inmate) wants by means of misleading or deceitful communication (Kauffman, 1988). Some inmates become so skilled and practiced at conning that they engage in what Bursten (1972) describes as manipulative cycling, characterized by a goal, an intent to deceive, the execution of the deceptive act, and a sense of triumph upon completion of the act. For example, consider this scenario:

> An inmate has just been "fired" as a janitor by the housing unit officer. The officer asked the unit counselor to reassign the inmate to another work area. The inmate, who enjoyed having the cell house to himself during the day, was determined to keep his job and decided to approach the associate warden whom he knew at another institution. He convinced the associate warden that he needed to remain in the unit because of safety concerns; he had been an assault victim at the previous institution. The associate warden instructed the counselor to leave the inmate's work assignment alone. On the following day, the inmate walked up to the unit officer and proudly announced that he was still a janitor.

Notice that the inmate experiences a sense of triumph after the officer's effort to fire him fails. Meloy (1988) observes that successful manipulation results in an emotional state that is rewarding to the manipulator. Unfortunately for staff, the "good con" (the successful duping of prison officials) simply requires careful thought and knowledge of the person being deceived.

Prison: An Ideal Context for Manipulation

Like it or not, inmate deception is an inevitable, predictable, and pervasive part of prison life. Certain fundamental realities are inherent in the prison environment, which encourage inmates to lie, manipulate, and otherwise deceive staff members. These include the built-in adversarial relationship between staff and inmates, power and control dynamics, the nature of the inmate subculture, and staff contributions to their own manipulation.

The Adversarial Relationship

Prisons are totalitarian communities where people are held against their will and forced to live with their keepers (Allen and Bosta, 1981). In other words, prison staff must contend on a daily basis with men and women who do not want to be in prison and who will do almost anything to make their time more comfortable and convenient. Inmates, therefore, can and should be expected to simultaneously resent staff for keeping them against their will, while relying upon them to a large extent for their survival and comfort. Such ambivalence creates optimal conditions for conning and deception.

Power Dynamics

Virtually all human relationships are characterized by a relative balance or imbalance in power (Schifter, 1999). Nowhere is this more apparent than in the relationship between a correctional employee and an inmate. Inmates are significantly powerless inasmuch as they are governed by voluminous and explicit rules and regulations which are vigorously enforced by staff. Moreover, inmates are subject to the threat of physical force if they choose to be noncompliant with staff direction. Assuming for a moment that all human beings have an inmate's need for power, as suggested by Glasser (2000), just how does an inmate manage to fulfill this need in an environment where he or she appears to have little or no control?

One way in which prisoners try to assert power is to dominate other inmates through threat, intimidation, and/or manipulation. Indeed, Benda, Corwyn, and Toombs (2001) observe that inmate peer associations are primarily based on manipulation and coercion. Another way is to engage in deception and manipulative behavior intended to undermine the authority and influence of the staff.

For example, the first author recalls an incident in a men's prison in which a no-nonsense if not overzealous correctional officer was writing an unprecedented number of disciplinary reports on inmates in his cell block. To say that the inmates were upset with this officer would be quite an understatement. However, there was little if anything they could do to remedy the situation since they had no choice but to comply with the officer's standards and expectations. Right? Wrong.

Some of the inmates staged a disturbance at the rear of the unit. While the officer went to investigate, an inmate smeared excrement over the earpiece of the telephone outside the housing unit office. When the officer returned to the office and picked up the phone to report the incident, his ear was instantly covered with feces. He was so traumatized by the incident that he was unable to work this particular housing unit for a long time. The perpetrators of this escapade were never identified.

Who had the power in this scenario? The reader is encouraged to remember that inmates will always try to find a way to restore the balance of power in their relationship with staff, and will go to great lengths and display remarkable creativity in their attempts to do so. Field (1994) refers to this as a disruption of the "normal asymmetry" of power in a conflict situation. In other words, the normally subordinate inmate acts as though he has become dominant and the staff member subordinate. Power-seeking manipulation can be most unpleasant to the staff member on the receiving end. Just ask the correctional officer who got an ear full of feces!

The Inmate Subculture

The inevitability of manipulation becomes even more obvious when one considers the nature and function of the inmate subculture and the beliefs, values, and "code" of behavior that characterize it. The inmate subculture has long captured popular as well as academic curiosity, principally because of the so-called "inmate code" and the dire consequences for those who deviate from it.

Kauffman (1988) identifies the basic elements of the inmate code:

1. Do not "snitch" on another inmate.
2. Do not cooperate or fraternize with the staff.
3. Maintain an appearance of solidarity.
4. Be loyal to fellow inmates.

Notice how adherence to these norms only serves to further polarize the staff and inmates which, as discussed earlier, gives rise to lying and manipulating. Moreover, Field (1994) observes that the inmate subculture values lying to authority, glorifying drugs and crime, and creating an atmosphere of negativism and pessimism. Such values encourage inmates to "get over" on or otherwise con staff.

The Staff Contribution

We have already noted that some degree of power imbalance exists in every human relationship. Each participant in the relationship, whether husband or wife, boss or employee, parent or child, or staff member or inmate chooses to accept, actively resist, or passively-aggressively resist the inequality in power and control. A passive-aggressive attempt to restore the balance in power between staff and inmates typically would involve some type of manipulation in which the staff member is deceived. In other words, a con is only successful if, in fact, someone is conned. Therefore, staff participate in manipulation by unwittingly playing a receptive role in the deception. A major objective of this book is to alert correctional staff to inmates' deceptive practices so that an employee can minimize his or her unintentional contribution to the process.

Many well-intended correctional employees unwittingly make themselves easy "marks" for inmate manipulation through misplaced acts of kindness or leniency. For example, a correctional counselor who permits an inmate to make a legal call, without first determining whether a compelling need for one actually exists, has just set himself up for similar requests from other inmates who learn about his "generosity."

Unfortunately, many inmates firmly believe that the world is divided into the strong and the weak (Schifter, 1999) and perceive leniency as a sign that the employee is "weak" and, therefore, exploitable. Prison staff also play an active role in their own victimization by inmate manipulation through their reactions to the discovery that they have been conned. For example, it is common for a correctional employee to become humiliated and enraged upon learning that he or she has been deceived. Some employees respond by trying to punish and retaliate against the inmate who successfully duped them. Unfortunately, such a "counterattack" usually backfires. For example, consider the following scenario:

> An inmate has just manipulated a food service foreman into allowing him to eat lunch early under the pretext of having left his "short line" pass in the housing unit. When the employee finds out later that the inmate is not authorized for the short line, he becomes irate and starts yelling and cursing at the inmates who work for him. One of them goes to the food service administrator who, in turn, directs the foreman to apologize to the inmate at whom he yelled. Consequently, the staff member not only finds himself the unsuspecting victim of an inmate con, but the recipient of a verbal reprimand from his boss as well!

Chapter 8 will offer a variety of guidelines and strategies to assist correctional employees in "damage control" after they have been duped by an inmate.

The Purposes of Inmate Deception

The time has come to address one of the core questions about inmate manipulation and deception. Simply stated, why do inmates con staff? For several reasons, the authors elect to reframe this question as the following: What is the purpose of inmate manipulation? "Why" questions, although intellectually stimulating, are ill-advised in the context of working with inmates. At best, they invite speculation and theorizing; at worst, they encourage the creation of excuses, rationalizations, and other justifications for deception. It is much more productive to examine the goals (the purpose) the inmate has in mind and/or the benefits (the payoff) he or she hopes to achieve as a result of conning staff.

Need Fulfillment

Perhaps the best starting point for examining the purpose of inmate manipulation is to acquaint the reader with the work of William Glasser, a psychiatrist whose 1965 book *Reality Therapy* emphasized the centrality of choice and personal responsibility in the genesis of criminal and delinquent behavior. Glasser (2000) has since asserted that virtually all human behavior represents an attempt by a person to meet one or more of five basic needs: love and belonging, power, freedom, fun, and survival. The individual chooses the behavior(s) which he or she believes is most likely to meet each need. Such a perspective is extremely helpful in explaining inmate manipulation, since the options available to inmates to meet their basic needs are certainly limited in a prison environment.

Love and Belonging

Some inmates will not hesitate to use or, more accurately, misuse staff members as they seek to satisfy their need for love and belonging. For example, it is not uncommon for inmates to seek frequent contact with opposite-gender staff members, often a counselor, psychologist, or chaplain, and concoct stories of woe to receive individualized attention from a man or woman. Other inmates may go further in this attempt to fulfill their need for love and belonging and actually try to develop a romantic or sexual relationship with a staff member. In Chapter 9, we present guidelines to help staff establish and maintain firm interpersonal boundaries with inmates.

Power and Control

There are innumerable ways in which inmates, who appear and claim to be virtually powerless (Aids Counseling and Education Program, 1998), endeavor to meet their need for power. The simplest and most basic method by which inmates try to control staff is to lie to them. Lying enables the inmate to control the impression he or she makes on staff, thereby increasing the likelihood of successful manipulation.

For example, an inmate recently told a prison psychologist that he had been sexually assaulted by two inmates. The alleged victim displayed the textbook symptoms of posttraumatic stress disorder. The psychologist immediately set in motion his agency's procedures for sexual assault intervention. Among other things, the inmate was placed in a special housing unit typically reserved for informants and other inmates who require close supervision or protection. Each inmate in this unit was housed by himself in a cell equipped with cable TV access. A lengthy and labor intensive investigation ultimately revealed that the inmate had not been sexually assaulted, but had been threatened with bodily harm because he had failed to pay off gambling debts.

It is important to understand that all attempts by inmates to exert power and control over staff share something in common. Such efforts reflect a view of staff as objects to be used toward self-serving ends and disregarded as human beings in their own right (Samenow, 1984). Moreover, like all deceivers, inmates feel contempt for the people they manipulate and exhilaration when the deceptions are successful (Gediman and Lieberman, 1996). Ekman (1992) refers to the sense of excitement associated with a successful con as "duping delight."

Understanding how inmates regard staff can be helpful in two ways. First, it alerts them to the fact that any inmate interaction bears the potential for deception and manipulation. Second, it makes it easier for the employee not to personalize an encounter in which he or she is successfully duped or conned by an inmate. We discuss the importance of not taking manipulation personally in Chapter 9.

Fun and Excitement

The general public assumes that prisons are monolithic, austere places where inmates, confined to their cells twenty-three or twenty-four hours per day, live in a regimented existence filled with boredom and monotony. In most prisons, nothing could be further from the truth. Indeed, even in so-called "supermax" institutions, in which inmates are "locked down" twenty-three hours per day, an array of opportunities are available—or created—whereby inmates can meet their need for fun.

For example, inmates will occasionally create disturbances just to see staff members run at top speed and otherwise "jump through hoops" to reach the site of the disturbance. The inmates involved in this deception find staff members responses to be highly entertaining. Marvin Zuckerman (2000) argues that people have a basic need for excitement and that, one way or another, they will fulfill it. Prison inmates are masters at generating their own excitement, often at the expense of well-meaning and unsuspecting staff members. Indeed, Allen and Bosta (1981) observe that inmates often develop elaborate and highly creative systems of deception for no other reason than their own pleasure.

Other Purposes

There are a number of other purposes served by inmate manipulation. For example, inmates will occasionally seek revenge against a staff member who they feel mistreated them. (Smearing feces on the telephone of a correctional officer perceived as overzealous in the performance of shakedowns is an excellent illustration of revenge-based manipulation.) Often inmates try to "get over" on staff to impress other prisoners and/or gain acceptance into a gang or clique. Still others engage in manipulation to "vent" feelings of anger and frustration which, if acted out, would result in assignment to disciplinary segregation. (The submission of frivolous grievances or lawsuits is a prime example of such indirect expression of anger and resentment.)

Inmates enrolled in treatment programs engage in all kinds of manipulation intended to divert staff from the task or curriculum at hand or, in the case of group therapy, avert confrontation and accountability (Sharp, 2000). In addition, some inmates will try to conceal their antisocial traits and create a favorable impression upon their counselor to gain a positive parole recommendation or the like (Salekin, 2000). Finally, inmates con and manipulate staff to support and maintain their criminal identity and lifestyle. This topic is the subject of the remainder of the chapter.

Manipulation as a Way of Life

The authors contend that inmate manipulation is best explained as a manifestation of an underlying antisocial belief system. Most inmates embrace a worldview that is strikingly different from that of law-abiding citizens. Research (Elliott, Fakouri, and Hafner, 1993) has shown that the fundamental views of life held by criminals and noncriminals are quite different. These differences are especially evident in the way in which criminals and noncriminals regard other people. Samenow (1984) has pointed out that criminals view other people as pawns on a chessboard; that is, other individuals exist only to fulfill the self-serving interests of the criminal. Criminals in confinement continue to display such an exploitative view of others by preying on prison staff members.

The Criminal Personality

The specific ways in which inmates view themselves, others, and the world are perhaps best described in considerable detail by Yochelson and Samenow (1976, 1977) who enumerated fifty-two "criminal thinking errors" which constitute the "criminal personality." The Yochelson and Samenow model, summarized and simplified by Samenow (1984), has become extremely popular among correctional counselors, probation and parole officers, and others who are involved in correctional treatment programs. However, this model suffers from a number of practical and conceptual problems. First, it lacks a theoretical basis: Yochelson and Samenow outline the mechanisms of criminal thinking, but do not explain its biological, psychological, or sociological underpinnings (Walters, 1990). Second, the sheer number of interrelationships among the thinking errors overwhelm both inmates who are trying to learn them and treatment staff who are endeavoring to teach them. Finally, Yochelson and Samenow's thinking is often unclear and unrelated to any of the major schools of psychological or criminological thought (Gacono and Meloy, 1988).

The Criminal Lifestyle

In his book, *The Criminal Lifestyle: Patterns of Criminal Conduct*, Glenn Walters (1990) expanded the Yochelson-Samenow model, retaining its central tenets while overcoming its aforementioned shortcomings. Walters (1990, 1994) asserts that antisocial behavior is initiated and supported by adherence to a set of eight criminal thinking patterns. The authors will demonstrate that the deception and manipulation which characterizes inmates' interactions with prison staff can be traced to one or more of the eight patterns. Indeed, each manipulative ploy described in Chapters 3 through 7 will be presented as an illustration of the prominent criminal thinking pattern on which it is based. First, however, a brief introduction to "lifestyle criminality" theory is warranted.

The Three Cs of Lifestyle Criminality

Walters' (1990) model of criminality regards crime and delinquency as a lifestyle based on three Cs: conditions, choice, and cognition. **Conditions** refer to the environmental and personal factors that place an individual at risk for future antisocial behavior (Walters, 1994). Examples of environmental conditions include peer group associates and family of origin, whereas personal conditions consist of such factors as temperament and intelligence. Although important, personal and environmental conditions are not considered causative factors in criminality. Rather, they serve to restrict or expand a person's options from which he or she makes a series of choices in regard to a given situation (Elliott and Walters, 1997).

Choice is not only of paramount importance in lifestyle criminality theory, but it is the cornerstone of the Yochelson-Samenow model as well. Walters (1990) and Samenow (1984) both agree that criminals choose to engage in antisocial behavior from an array of options, regardless of background, current life circumstances, or disability. Noncriminals, on the other hand, rarely consider crime as a problem-solving alternative. Indeed, Marek (2000) observes that people can be remarkably inventive in their efforts to cope with the most adverse and challenging conditions imaginable. For example, he describes the success of renowned psychologist Victor Frankl in finding purpose and meaning in his life while held captive in a Nazi concentration camp. Marek (2000) also notes that one's past, a personal condition in its own right, only influences behavior in a direction that is chosen.

Once a person has decided how he or she is going to handle a particular situation, it becomes necessary to live with those decisions. In other words, the individual must manipulate his or her thinking in such a way as to justify the choices made and protect them from external criticism. For the person who chooses to violate the law, this process gives rise to specific thinking patterns which form the centerpiece of the lifestyle model. **Cognition**, then, is the third "C" in Walters' (1990) triad.

There are eight cognitive patterns which serve to perpetuate the criminal lifestyle:

1. The Blaming Game or Mollification
2. Look at Me Being Good or Sentimentality
3. I'm in Charge or Power Orientation
4. That's Too Much Work or Cognitive Indolence
5. I Should Get What I Want or Entitlement
6. I Can Get By With Anything or Superoptimism
7. I Feel Nothing or Cutoff
8. I Talk One Way and Act Another or Discontinuity

We will describe these criminal thinking patterns in the following paragraphs.

1. "The Blaming Game" or Mollification involves an attempt by the criminal to transfer blame for his or her criminality to an external source (Elliott and Walters, 1997). Mollification assumes the form of excuses, justifications, rationalizations, or any other verbal explanation used by the criminal to mitigate responsibility or deny culpability for his or her criminal behavior. Yochelson and Samenow (1976) refer to such evasion of personal responsibility as the "victim stance;" to the criminal, he or she is the victim (of racial discrimination, persecution by the police, peer pressure, poor upbringing, and so forth), not the victimizer.

Many inmates who claim to have been physically abused as children approach the world from a victim's stance. They blame others for their problems rather than looking for solutions or making changes in themselves. No matter what they have done to or hurt other people, they try to make it look like they are the ones who have been injured. Playing the "excuse game" (Fautek, 2001) is such a deeply ingrained habit for most inmates that they tend to do it automatically. Indeed, inmates mollify their behavior so frequently that they come to believe that they can talk their way out of anything.

2. "Look at Me Being Good" or Sentimentality is defined as a criminal's attempt to present himself or herself in a favorable light despite a history of irresponsible, socially harmful behavior (Elliott and Walters, 1997). Whereas mollification entails the use of external conditions to justify criminal behavior, sentimentality typically involves a reference to a positive, socially redeeming action one has performed to divert attention from his or her more reprehensible behavior (Walters, 1990). Moreover, this cognitive pattern allows the criminal to deny the reality of his or her negative behavior and its impact on others (Walters and Elliott, 1999). This particular thinking pattern has been found to be especially prominent among female inmates (Walters, Elliott, and Miscoll, 1998).

3. "I'm in Charge" or Power Orientation is best described as the criminal's preoccupation with achieving a sense of power and control over his or her environment and the people in it (Walters, 1990). When the criminal does not feel in control of his or her immediate environment, he or she experiences what Yochelson and Samenow (1976) term the "zero state." Walters (1990) describes this state as an intense feeling of worthlessness and ineffectiveness. To escape such a feeling state, criminals engage in what Yochelson and Samenow (1976) call the "power thrust," whereby they strike out physically or verbally to regain a sense of control. In Chapter 4, the authors identify and discuss twelve ways in which inmates exhibit the power orientation in their interactions with staff.

4. "That's Too Much Work" or Cognitive Indolence refers to the criminal's quest for shortcuts to life's demands (Elliott and Walters, 1997). Indeed, Walters (1990) argues that the criminal seeks the path of least resistance in school, at work, and in virtually every other aspect of his or her life. Such mental laziness is a major cause of inmates' failure to complete prison treatment programs (Elliott and Walters, 1997). Cognitive indolence results from the criminal's low tolerance for boredom, concern with short-term rather than long-term solutions to problems, failure to challenge his or her own thinking, and inability to develop critical reasoning skills (Walters, 1994). Yochelson and Samenow's (1976) oft-cited observation that "the criminal is a sprinter, not a long distance runner" captures the essence of this thinking pattern.

5. "I Should Get What I Want" or Entitlement, according to Walters (1990), is a multifaceted thinking pattern whereby the criminal:

- Assumes ownership of anything and everyone he or she wants
- Embraces the belief that his or her uniqueness justifies doing whatever he or she wants to do
- Systematically misidentifies wants as needs

Most inmates consider anything they want to be something they must have (Fautek, 2001). This sense of entitlement enables the criminal to commit crimes, use drugs, and interfere with the private lives of others (Elliott andWalters, 1997). One clear sign of entitlement is an inmate's expression of outrage when a staff member denies a request or otherwise sets limits. It is as though inmates live by the motto, "Rules do not apply to me" (Bennett-Goleman, 2001).

6. "I Can Get By With Anything" or Superoptimism is defined by Walters (1990) as the criminal's unrealistic appraisal of his or her ability to achieve selected antisocial objectives. More specifically, superoptimistic thinking allows the offender to believe that he or she: 1) will escape detection; 2) if detected, will avoid apprehension; 3) if apprehended, will not be prosecuted; 4) if prosecuted, will not be found guilty; 5) if found guilty, will not go to prison; and 6) even if incarcerated, will be released early (Yochelson and Samenow, 1976). Samenow (1984) comments that superoptimism is the cognitive pattern that underlies "Big Score" thinking, in which the criminal gains more confidence and ups the ante after each crime he or she successfully perpetrates. The authors have found that many inmates lament the one "mistake" they made which led to their detection and conviction, and vow to "get it right next time." Superoptimism is also evident among inmates who begin treatment programs and believe that they will successfully change and remain permanently "rehabilitated" (Elliott and Walters, 1997).

7. "I Feel Nothing" or Cutoff is best described as a mental device which allows the criminal to immobilize the anxiety, guilt, fear, and other deterrents which would otherwise prevent him or her from committing a crime (Walters, 1990). There are as many forms of the cutoff as there are offenders, but this cognitive pattern typically consists of a word, phrase, visual image, or musical theme, which blocks out deterrents long enough for the criminal to commit a particular crime.

For example, many offenders find the phrase "fuck it!" to be especially useful in providing the impetus to move forward with criminal activity (Walters, 1990). Notice how this phrase is fueled with anger and hostility. Elliott and Walters (1997) point out that anger is very effective in purging the inmate's mind of deterrents to acting out.

The reader should also be aware that some criminals rely on alcohol or other drugs to quiet the inner voices that tell them not to engage in criminal behavior (Walters, 1994).

8. **"I Talk One Way and Act Another" or Discontinuity** refers to the inconsistency in thought and behavior regularly observed among criminal populations (Walters, 1990). As a consequence of this thinking pattern, offenders fail to follow through on initial commitments, carry out the requests of others, or remain focused on goals over time (Elliott and Walters, 1997). Discontinuity also involves a susceptibility to environmental events, which takes precedence over self-discipline; such distractability prevents the criminal from acting on initial good intentions (Walters, 1994). Prison inmates exhibit this thinking pattern every time they claim to embrace prosocial values, but then turn right around and commit a prohibited act.

For example, the first author recalls an incident involving an inmate who taught recovery classes in a residential substance abuse treatment program. It was determined that the inmate was smoking marijuana every night in a bathroom. When confronted on such hypocritical behavior, the inmate responded that what he did during his "free time" had absolutely nothing to do with his "job" (teaching the class).

The authors consider these eight criminal thinking patterns to be extremely useful in explaining the psychology of inmate deception and manipulation. Moreover, a thorough and precise understanding of these patterns will assist the correctional employee in quickly identifying a deceptive ploy and responding to it in a self-protective and professional manner. However, it is important for the reader to understand that these patterns seldom if ever occur in isolation from one another. Indeed, they tend to appear in combination with one or more patterns. For example, notice how many different thinking patterns are identifiable in the following vignette:

> Marcus (inmate) had submitted a cop-out (request form) to participate in a thirty-hour drug education program. He assumed (superoptimism) that he would be enrolled in the next class to

begin. When he discovered that his name was not on the enrollment list for the next class, he felt dejected and humiliated (power orientation: zero state). He approached the drug treatment specialist and demanded (entitlement) to know why his name had been excluded and argued that he (Marcus) was one of the few inmates who was really sincere about recovery (sentimentality). The treatment specialist explained that an inmate was enrolled in the program only if his case manager had referred him. Marcus was instructed to see his case manager to find out why he had not been referred. The inmate replied that it was not his responsibility (cognitive indolence) to pursue the matter and, even if he did, he would still remain excluded because the case manager did not like him (mollification). The treatment specialist told Marcus that there was nothing more to be discussed to which the inmate replied, "The hell with your drug program (cutoff). Who needs it anyway (discontinuity)? I'll just file a BP-9 (administrative remedy) to force (power orientation: power thrust) the case manager to explain why he didn't refer me in the first place."

Remarkably, all eight of Walters' (1990) criminal thinking patterns are evident in this fairly common scenario. Although one or more patterns may be emphasized, several others are operating behind the scene and in the examples of inmate manipulation continued in the next four chapters. Indeed, while describing the patterns one by one may help to clarify each of them, in real life they "often travel in packs and operate in clusters" (Gediman and Lieberman, 1996). Note that the eight criminal thinking patterns represent long-standing, deeply ingrained belief systems that are maintained even in the face of contradictory evidence (Padesky, 1994). Therefore, criminal thinking is extremely resistant to change and correctional employees should not expect inmates to be responsive to rational challenge. The importance of establishing realistic expectations concerning inmate behavior is discussed in Chapter 9.

PART II:
The Con Maneuvers

Chapter 3

Inmate Manipulation Based on a Sense of Entitlement

"I may be locked up, but I still deserve first-class treatment."

The previous chapter concluded with an overview of eight criminal thinking patterns, which, according to Walters (1990, 1994), initiate and maintain a criminal or substance-abusing lifestyle. The authors have observed that four of these patterns—entitlement, the power orientation, mollification, and sentimentality—are the principal driving forces behind the countless instances of deception and manipulation perpetrated by inmates against correctional staff every day. The current chapter is devoted to the illustration of "con jobs" based on entitlement. In Chapter 4, the authors examine twelve ways in which the power orientation is expressed through inmate attempts to deceive staff. Mollification is the featured criminal thinking pattern in Chapter 6, and in Chapter 7, the authors illustrate how sentimentality serves as the basis for deceptive and manipulative practices exhibited by many female offenders.

The reader will recall from Chapter 2 that entitlement is a multifaceted thinking error characterized by the 1) attribution of ownership over anything—or anyone—which the offender finds desirable; 2) a presumption of uniqueness—that is, the offender's belief that he or she is so special that privilege is a birthright; and 3) misidentification of desires or preferences as needs to be pursued at all cost (Walters, 1990). One or more of these components of entitlement is evident in many attempts by prison inmates to con staff members as illustrated in the scenarios which follow. Each vignette features a realistic portrayal of entitlement-based manipulation followed by a brief analysis in which we identify other prominent thinking patterns.

"I need a lay-in, Doc.
That job they've got me on is stressin' me out!"

David was an anxious, somewhat inadequate inmate who frequently presented the prison psychologist with a request for days off from work because he could not handle the "demands" placed upon him by his supervisor. The psychologist typically responded by offering support and encouragement, and then sent him back to his job in the prison laundry. On one occasion, while the psychologist was away from the institution, the inmate made the same request to the psychology intern but added a new twist: He complained that there was so little work to do in the laundry that his anxiety disorder was "flaring up" more than usual. David asked the psychologist to facilitate a reassignment to the prison factory where he could "keep busy and make more money." The intern, who was both surprised and impressed by David's newfound ambition, contacted the factory supervisor who agreed to place the inmate on the waiting list. David thanked the intern for his assistance and left the office, presumably to return to the laundry. An hour later, the intern received a call from the laundry supervisor who informed him that David had been placed in administrative detention because he had refused to return to work.

The inmate had reportedly left the psychologist's office and had gone straight to the lieutenant's office where he announced, "You'd better lock my ass up. There's no way in hell I'm goin' to work in the laundry while I'm on some damn waiting list!"

Analysis: In this vignette, David obviously considers himself to be so special or important (*uniqueness*) that he should not be expected to work at a job he regarded as aversive. Moreover, there is more than a hint that David had elevated his desire for the "ideal" job to the level of a need (*misidentification*): Just look at the effort he expended to get what he wanted. Finally, it appears as though he believed that he had the psychologists in his "hip pocket" (*ownership*) since he repeatedly turned to them for need fulfillment.

In addition to entitlement, David exhibits a host of other criminal thinking patterns. His desire to avoid hard work and frustration with being placed on a waiting list are reflective of cognitive indolence. The expectation that he could manipulate one psychologist into granting his request after another had declined to do so is suggestive of superoptimistic thinking. Mollification is implied in the inmate's quoted statement: He refers to the job "they have me on." In other words, it is "their" fault that he has to endure hardship at work. David's rapid shift from politeness (with the psychologist) to anger (in the lieutenant's office), coupled with his impulsive decision to be placed in administrative detention rather than return to work, is a prime example of the cutoff. Finally, his manipulation of one psychologist into granting his request after another had already denied it could have resulted in staff splitting, one of the twelve manifestations of the power orientation to be examined in Chapter 4.

"You gotta get me closer to home. My mama's sick and her doctor says it would help her to see me."

Anthony was a thirty-five-year-old federal prisoner of whom custodial and treatment staff alike were quite fond. His records indicated, and his behavior occasionally reflected, some mild mental retardation and a psychotic disorder. He displayed a childlike quality which treatment staff found most endearing. Correctional officers, on the other hand, admired Anthony's willingness to defend himself against physically stronger, predatory inmates. He routinely approached administrative officials and unit management staff at "main line" (noon meal) with a request for a transfer to either a medium-security institution or a medical center. However, the inmate's high custody/security classification score rendered him ineligible for a lower-security transfer, and the severity of his mental illness did not reach the threshold required for psychiatric in-patient treatment.

One morning Anthony paid a visit to his case manager and presented a most interesting and novel request. The inmate handed the staff member a letter from a physician in Anthony's hometown. According to the letter, the inmate's mother was seriously ill and it was the physician's professional opinion that proximity to her son might prove therapeutic. Interestingly, the doctor noted that the mother's condition was such that she could make the trip to a nearby federal prison for brief but frequent visits. The case manager, among the most experienced and competent at the institution, told Anthony that "hardship" transfers were rarely granted and that he doubted whether the inmate's situation would qualify. Nevertheless, the staff member, who like so many others found Anthony to be a sympathetic character, agreed to send the request "up the flagpole" for review. Remarkably, when a liberal "sliding scale" was used to evaluate Anthony's custody/security classification, it was determined that he met—albeit barely—the criteria for a lower-security transfer. It would not even be necessary to refer him for a hardship transfer! Six weeks later, Anthony was transferred to the medium-security prison located forty minutes from his mother's home.

Four months later, the case manager was summoned to the associate warden's office where he found the associate warden and case management coordinator eagerly awaiting his arrival. The coordinator informed the case manager that Anthony was "on his way back" because he had proved too difficult to manage at the medium-security institution. Moreover, the inmate had never received a visit from his mother who, upon discovering that her son was housed so near to her, had requested that her name be deleted from both his visiting and phone call lists. To add insult to injury, the case manager was advised that Anthony's mother was not in poor health nor was she ever a patient of the physician who had supposedly authored the letter. An investigation had revealed that the inmate had paid a former "cellie," now on parole, to type the letter on official-looking stationery and send it to Anthony in an envelope postmarked in his hometown.

The associate warden, both angry about and embarrassed by Anthony's successful attempt to "get over on my staff," asked the case manager why he did not verify the authenticity of the letter or the severity of the mother's alleged condition. The case manager responded, "Because, Boss, it was Anthony for Christ's sake! Who would have thought that he could have pulled off such a con?" The associate warden then turned to the case management coordinator and chastised her for being so "lenient" in scoring Anthony's custody/security classification.

Analysis: This vignette, like the previous one, features a multiplicity of criminal thinking patterns, all of which contributed to the "success" of Anthony's manipulation of not one but several staff members. First and foremost, the inmate evidenced a strong sense of entitlement: he regarded himself as so special and important (*uniqueness*) that he should be exempted from the established criteria for transfer to a lower-security institution. Additionally, Anthony viewed the case manager as someone whom he could place in his "corner" (*ownership*).

Finally, the inmate's insistence that he must be granted a transfer exemplified the escalation of a desire to a "need" (*misidentification*). The manner in which Anthony was able to use staff perceptions of him as a "sympathetic character" to his advantage is a fascinating illustration of sentimentality: he was able to induce staff to overlook his antisocial tendencies while instead focusing on his endearing qualities. The agility with which Anthony shifted from a supposedly hapless, mentally retarded, and/or psychotic individual to one who could wage battles against aggressive inmates is indicative of discontinuity. Still further, the inmate's ability to endear himself to staff and use outside resources to forge a letter from a physician are demonstrative of ingratiation and *sphere of influence*, respectively— two expressions of the power orientation to be discussed in Chapter 4.

"I'm not going to pay you people a dime toward victim restitution. You've already got me locked up, so there's not a damn thing more you can do to me!"

Steven, a twenty-four-year-old inmate just beginning a thirty-year federal drug sentence, appeared in front of his unit team for an initial classification hearing. He was asked by his counselor whether he was prepared to enroll in the Financial Responsibility Program through which fines, victim restitution payments, and other fees assigned by the sentencing judge are collected. Steven replied that he would enroll in the program as soon as he began working in the prison factory. His counselor gave him an application which he promised to complete and return the next day. Steven was admonished that he was expected to pay his rather substantial restitution assessment as soon as possible.

A month later, the counselor discovered that Steven had neither submitted a factory application nor enrolled in the Financial

Responsibility Program. Meanwhile, the inmate had been assigned as a housing unit orderly (janitor) by another counselor who was unaware of the earlier agreement. Steven was not the least bit concerned that he would be earning "a minimum wage;" he had more than $500 in his commissary account. When confronted on his failure to follow through on his commitment, Steven explained that he needed to spend every day in the law library to work on his appeal. The counselor reluctantly agreed to permit Steven to delay Financial Responsibility Program participation until his next unit team hearing in four months.

When Steven appeared before his team, he stated that he had no intention of working in the factory, citing such employment as "slave labor." He offered, with more than a touch of sarcasm, to allow the team to "take" the $5.25 he earned every month as an orderly. His unit manager informed Steven that he was on the verge of being placed in "Financial Responsibility Program Refusal" status, which would result in his ineligibility for transfer to another institution closer to home. Steven replied, with considerable contempt, by uttering the statement quoted above. That evening he completed the paperwork necessary to have all of the money in his commissary account sent home.

Analysis: Again, as in the previous vignette, uniqueness is reflected in the inmate's belief that he should be considered exempt from the policy requirements which apply to all inmates. Also, there is a strong sense that he regards his money to be just that: his money (*ownership*), even though a prescribed portion is to be paid into a victim compensation fund.

Mollification is embodied in his utter disregard for the victim who would stand to benefit from restitution; such crass insensitivity is indicative of the *denial of injury*, one of the "techniques of neutralization" described by Sykes and Mata (1970). The *victims' stance* (Yochelson and Samenow, 1976), another form of mollification, is implied in Steven's remark that "you've already got me locked up." At a more subtle level, the inmate manifests discontinuity in that he chooses not to do something—repay a debt—that he would not tolerate if done to him. In addition, there is an implied threat or chal-lenge in Steven's assertion that ". . . there's not a damn thing more you can do to me!" This is suggestive of extortion, another mode of expression of the power orientation to be described in Chapter 4.

"If you don't go in with me to see the 'board,' I don't stand a change of getting any play!"

Richard had completed approximately one-half of a residential drug treatment program when he was notified by his case manager that he was scheduled for a parole hearing in two months. This came as quite a surprise to the inmate who had hoped to complete the pro-gram prior to seeing the "board." Richard had almost completed the program at another institution where he had allegedly attempted to instigate a "food strike." There was insufficient evidence to support disciplinary action against him, but he was nevertheless transferred to his current institution for "administrative" reasons. He reasoned that his chances for a favorable outcome at the hearing were slim to none without evidence of drug program completion. He asked another inmate, who had been "down" for several years, for advice regarding anything he could do that might enhance his chances "with the board." The "old timer" suggested that he ask someone from the Psychology Department to serve as a "staff representative" at his hearing.

After a group session the following day, Richard asked Dr. Bates, the drug abuse program coordinator, if she would accompany him to his parole board hearing. She denied his request, explaining that there was nothing she could offer above and beyond the documentation of program participation which would already be available to board members. The inmate reiterated his request, imploring the coordi-nator to tell the board that he was sincere about recovery and was unlikely to recidivate. Dr. Bates politely but firmly replied, "I can't predict your future behavior and only time will tell whether or not you are committed to your recovery program." Richard knew that the quality of his program participation was mediocre at best, so he realized that he had better go to work on a "Plan B." Later that evening, he learned that Dr. Bates would be on vacation starting next week. His next "move" began to come into focus.

On the following Monday, Richard asked Mr. McCoy, one of the two drug treatment specialists, if he could have a word with him. Interestingly, Mr. McCoy was not the specialist to whose caseload Richard was assigned. The inmate had established a rapport with Mr. McCoy and knew that he was quite a hockey fan and an avid fisherman. Richard engaged the specialist in a lengthy conversation regarding both interests. When Mr. McCoy turned as if to leave, Richard initiated the following conversation:

Inmate:	"Mr. McCoy, any chance you'd be willing to put in a word for me with the parole board next week? It might make the difference in whether I get to leave a year or so earlier."
Mr. McCoy:	"Gee, I don't know. This is the first time somebody's ever asked me to do such a thing. Don't you think you'd be better off with Dr. Bates or Miss Godfrey (Richard's assigned treatment specialist)?"
Inmate:	"Dr. Bates is on vacation and I have to give my case manager the name of my representative this week. As for Miss Godfrey, I just don't feel that comfortable with her."
Mr. McCoy:	"Sure, why not? Tell your case manager to put my name down."

Two months later, Mr. McCoy honored his agreement to represent Richard at the parole hearing.

In response to direct questioning, the treatment specialist characterized the inmate's participation as "above average" and confirmed that he was "on course" for program completion. Parole board members expressed concern over the discrepancy between Mr. McCoy's evaluation and that contained in the documentation. However, by a vote of two-to-one, board members granted Richard a six-month time cut for "superior programming." The inmate thanked Mr. McCoy for "going to bat" for him and returned to the unit where he bragged that he was the first inmate to receive such a "cut" in three years. He also told the inmates that Mr. McCoy's presence at the hearing "made all the difference in the world."

The next morning, Dr. Bates was inundated with requests to represent them at various parole, clemency, or classification hearings. Meanwhile, Miss Godfrey was asked why she had not represented Richard since she was his primary treatment specialist. At a staff meeting that afternoon, both women registered their displeasure and irritation with Mr. McCoy who apologized and stated, "I didn't know that it would be such a big deal." Dr. Bates reprimanded Mr. McCoy for failing to seek supervisory guidance in the matter, and instructed both treatment specialists to deny all future inmate requests for assistance with or appearances at parole hearings.

Analysis: This scenario is a virtual textbook illustration of entitlement: First, Richard's belief that he should be even considered for parole speaks to his sense of *uniqueness*; after all, he had not yet completed a drug treatment program and had been suspected of masterminding a disturbance at another institution. Second, *ownership* of the drug treatment staff is implied by his insistence that one of them must represent him at the hearing. Third, his persistence and ingenuity in securing such representation are clear evidence of the *misidentification* of a desire (staff assistance) as a need. Moreover, Richard's expectation that the program coordinator would be able or willing to proclaim that he is at low risk to recidivate is a testament to his superoptimistic thinking.

The astute reader will discern indications of cognitive indolence and discontinuity in Richard's admittedly mediocre program performance with so much at stake. In addition, mollification is suggested by his insinuation that the drug treatment specialist—not Richard—is ultimately responsible for the outcome of the hearing. Finally, the power orientation is expressed through his employment of ingratiation (talking about sports with Mr. McCoy) and staff *splitting* (creating tension and conflict between Mr. McCoy and the other two members of the treatment team).

"Please let me call home. I haven't heard from my wife in three weeks and I know something's wrong."

Dominic had been released on parole supervision after serving eight years in prison for an assault and battery conviction in which his ex-wife was the victim. Shortly before his release, he had married a woman whom he had met via correspondence. She was also divorced and had three children. Six months after he was released from prison, Dominic was found to have violated the conditions of his parole after police were called to his home to investigate an anonymous complaint that he was physically abusing his new wife. The officers found Dominic's wife seriously injured and in need of hospitalization. She told them that this was the worst of several beatings she had received from her husband. Dominic, who had left before the police arrived, was arrested an hour later in a tavern he routinely frequented. A month after his return to prison, Dominic approached his counselor with the request quoted above. The counselor, who had known the inmate during his earlier period of confinement, found Dominic to be likeable and rather entertaining. He suggested that the inmate write a letter to his wife or to other family members who might have information concerning her welfare.

Dominic replied that he had already written several letters to which he had received no response and, moreover, he had no money for stamps. The counselor offered to give him a few stamps, but Dominic insisted that it was important that he speak to her over the phone so that "I can hear her voice and know in my heart that she is all right." The counselor acquiesced and agreed to place the call at once. After three unsuccessful attempts to reach Dominic's wife, the counselor made arrangements with a colleague to try that evening.

The next day, Dominic's counselor was summoned to his unit manager's office. The unit manager explained that he had received a call from the inmate's former parole officer who reported that Dominic was making "harassing" phone calls to his wife. The counselor stated that he did not know what the parole officer was talking about. The unit manager handed the counselor a memorandum written by the latter's colleague the night before. The memorandum documented that Dominic had demanded money from, made accusations toward, and shouted obscenities at his wife. At no time during the conversation did the inmate inquire as to his wife's health and welfare. The phone call was terminated after other inmates complained that Dominic was talking so loudly that they couldn't carry on their own telephone conversations. The unit manager chastised the counselor for having authorized the call in the first place, and advised him that Dominic's wife had placed a "block" on her phone to prevent any future calls from the inmate.

Analysis: A sense of entitlement is evident both in Dominic's interaction with his counselor and his abusive relationships with his ex-wife and current wife. There is a desperate, pleading quality to his request for an emergency phone call, which is suggestive of the *misidentification* of a desire as a need. His expectation that the counselor would grant him a call outside the parameters of normal procedures indicates that Dominic considered his situation to be so special or important (*uniqueness*) that such an accommodation was warranted. Dominic's abusive behavior toward both his former and current wife offers a particularly vivid illustration of the *ownership* component of entitlement. Indeed, violence perpetrated by an abuser toward his partner usually indicates that he regards her as his "property" and expects her to fulfill his every need or want (Dutton, 1995). Physical violence notwithstanding, the demanding and degrading manner in which Dominic spoke with his wife over the phone is further evidence of a sense of *ownership*.

Dominic's successful manipulation of his counselor is replete with several criminal thinking patterns besides entitlement. His self-reported lack of funds and unwillingness to wait for a response to the letters he claimed to have written are demonstrative of cognitive indolence. One can infer sentimentality from his self-presentation as a devoted, concerned husband when he made his initial request. Dominic's declaration that he wanted "to hear her voice and know in my heart that she is all right" is blatantly discontinuous with the verbal abuse he directed toward her over the phone. Finally, the inmate's ability to "entertain" the counselor and thereby curry favor is yet another expression of the power orientation through ingratiation.

"If you had to spend just one night in this hell hole, you'd never even think about turning down the air conditioning!"

Lamont had already established quite a reputation as a "whiner" by the time he enrolled in a residential drug abuse treatment program. He was such a chronic complainer that staff and inmates alike found him to be annoying. Nevertheless, the inmate met the eligibility criteria for program participation and qualified for a sentence reduction of up to one year for successful program completion. Lamont was placed in a group of inmates to which Mr. Grover was the assigned drug treatment specialist. Classes met in a refurbished classroom in which a window-mounted air-conditioning unit had recently been installed.

The Drug Abuse Program Coordinator, Dr. Bennett, sat in on one of Mr. Grover's classes one morning and found that she had considerable difficulty following the group discussion because of the noise generated by the air conditioner. She walked over to the unit and turned it down, much to Lamont's chagrin. He angrily complained, "This is the only time of day we get to cool off. You people (staff) get to sit in air conditioning all day." Dr. Bennett quietly but firmly redirected Lamont's and the other inmates' attention to the lesson Mr. Groves was presenting. After class Dr. Bennett chastised Lamont for having momentarily disrupted class. The inmate reiterated his position that the air conditioner should remain on high "because most of us guys work in the factory all day." Dr. Bennett replied, "I had difficulty hearing the discussion and I'm quite certain that others did, too. Besides, the room is still comfortable even when the air conditioner is set on low. From now on, the air conditioner will remain on low during class."

Mr. Grover witnessed the interaction between Lamont and Dr. Bennett. At the beginning of class the next day, Lamont raised his hand and proclaimed, "Mr. Grover, us guys were talking last night and we don't think it's right that Dr. Bennett comes in here and changes the way we do things. It's your class. You set the rules." When asked by the specialist for clarification and elaboration, Lamont stated, "Like yesterday. She just comes in here and turns down the air conditioner 'cause she says people can't hear. None of us had a hard time hearing, so it must be just her. Maybe she ought to get a hearing aid or something." He then turned to the rest of the class and asked, "Ain't that so guys?" Several inmates shook their heads in the affirmative while others openly expressed their desire for maximum coolness. Mr. Grover, clearly uncomfortable with the discussion, stated, "Okay. Here's what we'll do. We'll turn the air conditioner on high unless Dr. Bennett is in the room. Now, I don't want to hear any more about this." Always one to have the final word on a subject, Lamont uttered the statement quoted at the beginning of this vignette.

Two weeks later, the chief psychologist entered the classroom to make an announcement regarding an upcoming graduation ceremony for another group. He asked Mr. Grover to turn down the air conditioner and commented that it was quite noisy. The chief psychologist later mentioned his concern about the noise level of the air conditioner to Dr. Bennett who was most displeased to learn that the unit was still being run on "high." She met with Mr. Grover later in the day and rebuked him for failing to comply with her direction that the air conditioner be kept on "low" during class.

Analysis: A host of criminal thinking patterns is apparent in this scenario, any one of which could be considered prominent. However, it is Lamont's sense of entitlement to the comfort of maximum air conditioning which serves as the driving force behind the manipulation of the drug treatment specialist. The inmate clearly *misidentified* his preference for a cool room temperature as a need that must be fulfilled. His relentless demand that the air conditioner be set at the temperature which he deemed appropriate is suggestive of a sense of *ownership* over the air conditioner. (Over the years, the authors have been both amused and amazed at the extent to which inmates have assumed "ownership" of chairs, tables, fans, televisions, and other items purchased by the government for all inmates.)

Lamont's unwillingness to endure the "hardship" of a less than ideally cool room temperature is typical of the low frustration tolerance associated with cognitive indolence. The fact that he is enrolled in a drug abuse treatment program, yet is more concerned about room temperature than the instructor's presentation, is indicative of discontinuity. Lamont's statement that, "If you had to spend just one night in this hell hole" implicitly blames staff for creating an adverse condition (heat) and allowing it to persist. This is a subtle example of a specific type of mollification to which Sykes and Matza (1970) refer as "condemning the condemners." Finally, the power orientation is expressed in two ways: First, Lamont invokes the power of group solidarity when he gains support for his "cause" from other inmates in the class. Second, he successfully engages in staff *splitting* when he cons Mr. Grover into disregarding Dr. Bennett's instructions regarding the air conditioner setting.

"Look here, I've spent the last three years locked down, and I've had a single cell everywhere I've been. I'm not going to take a cellie here!"

Jorge was a physically strong and otherwise imposing inmate who had spent the last three years confined in a "supermax" prison where he was isolated from both staff and inmates. He had an extensive history of assaulting staff and had killed another inmate several years ago. The inmate made the above quoted remark immediately upon admission into the receiving and discharge area of the penitentiary which was to be his new "home." A procession of institutional staff, including the captain, the chief psychologist, and even an associate warden attempted to persuade Jorge into celling with another inmate who was guaranteed to be "compatible." However, the inmate remained adamant in his position that he would cell with no one and stated that if forced into an occupied cell, "I'll have no choice but to hurt the guy." After two hours of futile negotiation, the decision was made to place Jorge in a cell by himself in the special housing unit until the warden could be consulted.

Since the special housing unit was already crowded, it was necessary to release two inmates into the general population before they had completed their prescribed period of disciplinary segregation. Jorge was the subject of a lengthy discussion at the segregation meeting a few days later. Some staff recommended that the inmate be returned to the supermax prison from which he had come, while others suggested that he be assigned a single cell for a while to facilitate his adjustment to a more open environment than the one he had just left. The warden, who was in attendance, asserted that he did not want to establish a precedent that anybody transferred from a supermax facility would be accorded single cell status. Moreover, he directed that Jorge be informed that he would take a cellie if he had any intention of entering the general population.

Upon conclusion of the meeting, the special housing unit lieutenant went to Jorge's cell and informed him of the warden's decision. The inmate replied, "Fuck it, then I'll just stay out here and lay down." The lieutenant responded, "Hey, man, why don't you at least give it a shot? You've already been locked down for three years." Jorge stared at the lieutenant and then said, "Look, you people do what you gotta do, and I'll do what I need to do. This conversation is over."

Analysis: Jorge's demand that he be housed in a cell by himself represents a classic illustration of entitlement. First, his sense of *uniqueness* is implied by his contention that, as a former supermax inmate, he deserves a single cell. The authors have noted that such inmates often regard themselves as "convicts," who adhere to a sacred code of "honor," rather than ordinary "inmates." Second, Jorge's reference to the fact that he has enjoyed a single cell assignment for three years suggests that he assumes *ownership* of this status. Third, the intensity and persistence with which the inmate insists that he must be celled alone clearly indicates that he has *misidentified* a privilege as a right. In addition, his expectation of single cell assignment immediately upon arrival at a new institution reflects superoptimism.

Jorge is one who relies heavily on *extortion* as his preferred approach to expressing the power orientation. Initially, he threatens to harm a prospective cellie; he then implies that he will refuse to enter the general population and remain in special housing unless he is housed alone. The inmate engages in the cutoff when he exclaims, "Fuck it, then. I'll just stay out here and lay down." As mentioned in Chapter 2, the use of this expression, fueled by anger and indignation, is one of the most common forms of the cutoff (Walters, 1990). Finally, a subtle display of mollification is evident in Jorge's assertion that he has "no choice" but to hurt a prospective cellie; the insinuation, of course, is that staff would be to blame if someone were hurt.

"I've got to stay here. My services are needed in the kosher kitchen."

Marshall, who will be reintroduced later in the book, was a bank robber who had served time in three different federal penitentiaries. He had finally become eligible for redesignation to a medium-security institution, and his case manager had already begun the paperwork necessary to for a transfer. However, Marshall was adamantly opposed to the idea of a transfer because he had carved out a very comfortable niche for himself at his current institution. His work assignment was that of a cook for the "kosher kitchen," a small section of the food service department devoted to preparing meals for Jewish inmates. He "earned" quite a bit of money by taking food out of the dining hall and selling it to other inmates throughout the prison. The inmate knew that he would be forced to work at a "real job" if he were transferred to a medium-security facility.

Marshall pleaded with his case manager to permit him to remain at the penitentiary. "My services are needed in the kosher kitchen." The case manager explained that the inmate was no longer eligible for placement in a high-security institution. Marshall "took his case" to the warden who declined to make an exception to the classification policy. The inmate was just about to call his girlfriend and give her the "bad news" that he was being transferred to a less secure prison when he noticed something on the bulletin board in his unit: The psychology department was sponsoring a "criminal personality" course open to all inmates. Marshall smiled to himself, certain that he had found a solution to his dilemma.

The next morning, Marshall paid a visit to the first author—the psychologist who was offering the course—and presented him with a box filled with certificates, lesson plans, and other materials pertaining to a "criminal personality" course, which the inmate claimed to have "taught" at his previous institution. The author was extremely impressed with Marshall's knowledge and enthusiasm, and asked him if he would like to co-instruct the course. The inmate replied that he would like nothing better, but explained that he would be transferred within a matter of weeks. The author, who believed that Marshall would prove indispensable to the success of the new course, convinced the case management coordinator to assign a "management variable" thereby enabling Marshall to remain at the penitentiary. (The author later regretted this action, but that is a story for another book!)

Analysis: Marshall presents to the reader a vintage illustration of entitlement: The inmate's remark that his "services are needed in the kosher kitchen" implies that he is indispensable and speaks volumes about his sense of *uniqueness*. His self-promotion as an "expert" in the "criminal personality" is a further testament to his inflated sense of self-importance (*uniqueness*). He personally attended to all facets of the operation of the kosher kitchen, "running" it as if it were his personal business enterprise (*ownership*). The determination with which he sought to circumvent classification policy is evidence that he felt that he "needed" to remain at the penitentiary, rather than merely preferring to do so (*misidentification*).

Marshall's confidence that he could find a way out of his dilemma is indicative of superoptimism, while his aversion to the assignment of a "real job" exemplifies cognitive indolence. Marshall expressed the power orientation in two ways. First, he engages in negotiation (*see*

49

Chapter 4) with the author by agreeing to co-instruct the course only if, of course, he could remain at the penitentiary. Second, his ability to "dazzle" the author with his knowledge of and enthusiasm for a subject of interest to the latter is an example of ingratiation. Finally, Marshall's presumption that he could teach a course on "The Criminal Personality" to inmates while still engaging in illicit behavior (stealing food from the kosher kitchen) is demonstrative of discontinuity.

"Since I was able to help you out, there is something you can do for me."

David Lewis-Bey was an inmate who regularly attended Nation of Islam services and spent a large portion of his "free" time in the prison chapel. He often volunteered to help the chaplain inventory donated items and distribute greeting cards to the inmate population. David "took charge" of issuing cassette tape players which inmates used to listen to musical, meditative, or religious audio-tapes. The chaplain was grateful for David's assistance and allowed him to remain in the chapel until count time every evening. Unbeknownst to the chaplain, however, the inmate was taking a tape player and selected tapes to his housing unit every evening. He would "permit" other inmates to listen to tapes in their cells in exchange for various commissary items.

David was careful to "return" the tape player and tapes to the chapel the following morning. On a morning when the institution was on "lock down" status because of fog conditions, the chaplain decided to conduct a long overdue equipment inventory. He discovered that one of the tape players was missing and assumed that it had to be misplaced. After all, David did a magnificent job tracking and monitoring the use of the tape players. After the fog lifted and the count cleared, David headed straight for the chapel to replace the player and tapes.

When the chaplain unlocked the chapel door for David, he told the inmate that one of the tape players appeared to be missing. He asked for David's assistance in finding the item and expressed concern that failure to do so could result in discontinuation of the program. David replied that he was certain that all of the tape players had been returned last evening and promised to locate the missing one. David "searched" for the tape player for approximately twenty-five minutes before he proudly informed the chaplain that he had found it wrapped in some Muslim prayer rugs. The chaplain, both relieved and grateful, remarked that the associate warden would have been very upset if "another piece of equipment came up missing." David responded, "I'm glad I could come to the rescue, Chaplain." The inmate paused for a moment, and then said, "Since I was able to help you out, there is something you can do for me."

Analysis: We can see David's sense of entitlement in a number of ways in this scenario. First, he assumed *ownership* of not only the issuance of tape players and tapes, but of the items themselves. The equipment became David's property rather than that of the chapel. Second, he *misidentifies* the performance of a "good deed" as an extraordinary gesture worthy of a reward rather than something which responsible people do in the spirit of altruism. Third, one can infer a sense of uniqueness from the importance and otherwise "special" status that David enjoys as the one "in charge" of issuing the tapes and tape players.

The power orientation is expressed in at least two ways in this vignette. First, David's ability to make himself so valuable to the chaplain is an example of *ingratiation*. Second, the "Now that I've scratched your back, you can scratch mine" quality of his request for a favor is demonstrative *of negotiation*. David's self-promotion as a "rescuer" exemplifies the "helluva fella" (Walters, 1990) dimension of sentimentality. Obviously, the mere fact that he would misappropriate and use items for illicit purposes—from the very place where he attends worship services—is a classic illustration of discontinuity. However, perhaps the most striking display of criminal thinking is to be found in the superoptimism and discontinuity inherent in David's distorted belief that he should be rewarded for returning something that he himself had stolen.

"Your staff promised that they'd get me closer to home. They lied! Now, what am I supposed to tell my people?"

Peter was a member of the first group of inmates to complete a residential values program at a federal penitentiary. One of the incentives for program participation was the possibility of a transfer to an institution closer to the inmate's home. Peter had talked of nothing but "getting back home" since his acceptance into the program. Treatment staff and his case manager had cautioned the inmate that he might not necessarily be transferred to the specific prison of his choice; it was more likely that he would be redesignated to an institution in the region of the country in which his home was located. Nevertheless, Peter instructed his family to relocate from the midwestern city, where the penitentiary was located, to a small town in the Pacific Northwest nearby the prison to which the inmate expected to be transferred. Four weeks later, Peter approached his case manager and inquired about the status of his transfer. The staff member checked his computer and informed the inmate that he had been redesignated to a newly opened institution in southern California. Peter flew into a rage and angrily exclaimed, "That's bullshit! You people lied to me. You're not going to get away with this!"

The case manager admonished the inmate to calm down and explained to him that a moratorium had been placed on transfers to the institution in the Pacific Northwest, and reminded Peter that he would still be much closer to his home than he was at present. The inmate indignantly denounced the case manager's explanation and demanded to call his family at once. The case manager declined the request and told the inmate to leave his office.

At noon "main line," Peter approached the warden and forcefully alleged that he had been "deceived" by the program staff who had "promised" him a transfer closer to home. The inmate proceeded to enumerate his many contributions to the program for which he had neither sought nor received acknowledgment. He claimed to have designed the program's logo and painted it at the entrance to the unit, assisted "slower" inmates with homework assignments, and helped program staff translate handout materials from English to

Spanish. The warden commended Peter for his efforts, but reiterated the case manager's response that a moratorium had been placed on transfers to the desired institution. The inmate replied, "Your staff promised that they'd get me closer to home. They lied! Now, what am I supposed to tell my people?" The warden, concerned that Peter's disillusionment and resentment might be "contagious" within the program, agreed to intervene on the inmate's behalf.

Analysis: This vignette is an appropriate one with which to conclude the chapter since it prominently depicts all eight of the criminal thinking patterns identified by Walters (1990, 1994). First, and perhaps foremost, the inmate clearly "pushes the envelope" with his sense of entitlement. His belief in his own *uniqueness* is verified by his contention that he should be transferred to the institution of his choice even though a moratorium had been placed on all transfers there. In addition, an attitude of *ownership* is apparent since he acted as if the transfer were in his possession from the beginning of his tenure in the program. Peter's insistence that he was being deprived of a transfer that he had been promised reflects the *misidentification* of a possibility as a certainty. The inmate's demand that the case manager call his family and the implicit threat contained in his statement, "You're not going to get away with it!" are, of course, manifestations of the power orientation. Peter's recitation of the many contributions he made to the program exemplifies sentimentality.

Peter's insinuation that his family would suffer because of program staff's "deception" is illustrative of mollification. His choice to hear only what he wanted to hear, rather than attend to the case manager's caveat regarding what was meant by "closer to home," and his impulsiveness and prematurity in telling his family to relocate, all reflect cognitive indolence. The absolute certainty with which he regarded the approval of a transfer to the desired institution is indicative of superoptimism. The cutoff was expressed through the abrupt and anger-laden manner in which he said, "That's bullshit! You people lied to me." Discontinuity was exhibited in at least two ways. First, he failed to consider the fact that he placed his family in the position of having to relocate simply by committing the crime which resulted in his incarceration. Instead, he objects to the inconvenience his family must endure because of classification decisions. Second, Peter's outrage at being denied something to which he felt entitled and the threats and demands he registered are hardly compatible with the notion of tolerance, one of the four "core values" to which the program was anchored.

Chapter 4

Inmate Manipulation Based on the Power Orientation

"I may be locked up, but I'm still in charge."

Inmates' interactions with other people are often adversarial and dominated by a quest for power and control, which Walters (1990, 1994) refers to as the power orientation. For many offenders, "cooperation is seldom more than a passing convenience" (Gornik, 2001, p. 61). A "win-lose" orientation dominates many inmates' interpersonal relationships. To these inmates, the only way to really win is to force someone else to lose. The sense of triumph that results from this kind of "winning" is the only way such offenders have learned how to achieve personal satisfaction from their interpersonal relationships. Nowhere are inmates' efforts to win—by defeating others—more apparent than in their day-to-day interactions with correctional staff.

The vignettes presented in this chapter feature twelve common ways in which inmates attempt to wield power and control over staff. We present three different examples of these power-orientation strategies. Each of the first set of vignettes is preceded by a formal definition of the featured power and control strategy. The remaining vignettes are followed by a brief commentary in which specific dimensions of the power orientation are identified.

Testing

Testing refers to an effort to create a situation in which an inmate can gather information about a staff member or a group of staff. Once the "test results" are in, the inmate "files" the information away for use at a later date. For example, inmates often create situations to determine if a new correctional officer will tend to be lenient or vigilant in the enforcement of rules and regulations. If it is discovered that the employee is one who "goes by the book," they will be more discrete in their commission of prohibited acts.

Inmates participating in treatment programs will sometimes disclose relatively unimportant information to their therapist with a request for privacy and confidentiality. If they uncover evidence that the clinician may have "leaked" the information to a third party, they will divulge nothing of a meaningful or sensitive nature throughout the course of treatment. Testing is usually a prelude to other power and control-based manipulation. However, it provides a sense of "duping delight" (Ekman, 1992) in its own right because the employee is often unaware that he or she has either "passed" or "failed" a test.

****

During a group therapy session at a women's prison, one of the group members disclosed that she felt "like killing" another offender in her housing unit. The group worked hard with the offender to show her that such feelings of anger and thoughts of violence were counterproductive and incompatible with her goal of a record of clear conduct. At the conclusion of the session, the group therapist, a neophyte behavioral clinician, called her supervisor, a first-year psychologist, and informed her that one of the offenders in the group might be "homicidal." The clinician related the statement that the offender had made and the psychologist instructed her to call the shift supervisor and request that the offender be placed in secure quarters as a possible "threat to others."

The following week, three offenders announced that they wanted to withdraw from the group because they could not trust the behavioral clinician. One of the women expressed outrage that the therapist had "snitched out" their peer thereby prompting her placement in "lock" (secure quarters). The clinician, who felt attacked and perplexed, replied, "You ladies know that I am obligated to report any possibility of violence or escape!" To this, another offender responded, "Look, Miss Rivers, if you call custody every time one of us says we feel like killing somebody, we'll all be locked up! Besides, Bertha (the offender placed in secure quarters) just said that to see if you could be trusted. I guess we all found out, didn't we?" A third offender remarked that "Bertha wouldn't hurt a flea. She told us before the group that she was going to throw you some bait and see if you'd bite."

The three vocal offenders stood in unison and left the group room vowing never to return. During the ensuing week, the remaining five members also withdrew from the group. (This is an illustration of solidarity, another expression of the power orientation to be examined later in this chapter.) Ms. Rivers' supervisor, who accepted part of the responsibility for the demise of the group, commented, "I guess they gave us a test, and we flunked it."

Diversion

Diversion refers to any tactic designed to divert a staff member's attention or focus in order to indulge in prohibited behavior or achieve some other secondary gain. Diversionary tactics used with correctional officers often involve the creation of a minor disturbance by one or more inmates which compels an officer to abandon a supervisory post to investigate the incident. Meanwhile, another inmate or group of inmates engages in nefarious activity. In counseling and treatment contexts, diversion typically involves an attempt to defocus the counselor or teacher from the lesson or issue under discussion, thereby enabling an inmate to avoid the "hot seat" or permitting a class or group of offenders to "slack off."

****

Keith was one "strike" away from being expelled from a drug education class. He had already received a verbal warning and a written notice from the drug treatment specialist regarding his unwillingness to participate in class discussions and failure to complete a homework assignment, respectively. The treatment specialist had established a solid reputation as a "no-nonsense" instructor who rigidly adhered to a "three strikes and you're out" approach to running his classes. At the beginning of class one day, the specialist announced that he was going to administer a "pop quiz" over some reading material he had passed out the week before. Keith had not bothered to even look at the material and knew at once that he would fail the quiz and thus be expelled from the class.

Shortly after the quiz was distributed, Keith raised his hand and told the specialist that he was experiencing sharp pains in his chest. He added that his father had died from a heart attack at age fifty-two. The specialist, skeptical but not one to ignore a potentially serious medical complaint, contacted health services by radio and was instructed to send the inmate to the infirmary at once. As he left the classroom, Keith turned to the specialist and asked, "What about my quiz?"

The specialist replied, "Don't worry about it right now. We'll work something out next week." The inmate thanked the staff member for his kindness and understanding and departed for the infirmary where, of course, no basis for his chest pains was discovered.

Extortion

Extortion refers to any measure employed by an inmate that is intended to threaten, intimidate, or otherwise coerce a staff member into doing something, which the employee does not want to do. Inmates will occasionally be obvious in their attempts to extort favors from staff. For example, an inmate might say to a case manager, "If you don't give me a single cell, I'll fuck up my cellie." This creates quite a dilemma for the staff member. He or she has a choice between reinforcing the inmate's sense of entitlement or possibly jeopardizing the safety of another inmate. Much more common, however, are subtle attempts by inmates to influence staff behavior through extortion.

* *

The first author recalls his initial interaction with a state boarder several years ago. After mutual introductions, the inmate looked directly at the author and suggested, "Doc, you might be interested in seeing what happened the last time I talked to a shrink." The author, although somewhat disquieted by the sinister quality of the inmate's statement, proceeded with a standard and uneventful psychological examination. Later that day, the author reviewed the inmate's central file and found that the inmate had physically assaulted a psychologist in a state facility after the psychologist had solicited an early childhood memory concerning the inmate's mother.

Disreputation

Disreputation refers to an inmate's attempt to undermine the authority of staff members by calling into question their credibility, integrity, or expertise. This form of the power orientation is intended to discredit employees to such an extent that they become ineffective in the performance of their official duties. In most cases, the inmate bears no particular malice toward the employee whom he or she attempts to discredit; rather, the offender merely seeks to achieve a sense of superiority over the staff member.

****

Ten years ago, an inmate committed suicide in the special housing unit of a maximum security prison. Earlier in the day, he had been evaluated by the first author who found no evidence of mental illness or suicidality. For the next several weeks, another inmate who resided in the same unit challenged the author's credentials and clinical skills. The inmate denounced the psychologist's competence each time he made rounds in the unit. On one occasion, as the first author was attempting to conduct monthly mental health reviews, the inmate loudly discouraged other inmates housed on the same range from cooperating with the reviews. The other inmates joined in the derision of the author and other staff responded to the escalating noise and chaos. The author was asked to cease making rounds in special housing until his vocal "critic" was transferred to another institution.

Negotiation

Negotiation refers to an inmate's offer to exchange something of value to staff, such as information regarding a planned escape, for something of value to the inmate. This "quid pro quo" arrangement ostensibly appears to be a "win-win" proposition. However, as noted earlier in this chapter, most inmates are only interested in transactions in which they are the clear winners. In so-called negotiation, the offender "bargains" for something to which he or she would ordinarily not be entitled. Moreover, the inmate usually strives to obtain considerably more in the "deal" than he or she gives.

****

The first author was approached by a penitentiary inmate who claimed to have "proof" that an employee was bringing in expensive tennis shoes and selling them to inmates. The author referred the inmate to the institution's criminal investigator, but the offender insisted that he needed to speak directly to the warden. Much to the author's surprise, the warden, who had suspected the employee of "trafficking," agreed to meet with the inmate. However, before the inmate offered the "proof" of the staff member's impropriety, he requested a transfer to a lower security institution, preferably one closer to home. The warden agreed to facilitate such a transfer, even though the inmate's custody-security classification score warranted placement in a penitentiary. In addition, the inmate was granted immunity from disciplinary proceedings for his role as the "distributor" of the contraband items.

Rumor Clinic

The rumor clinic refers to an inmate's dissemination of information, or more frequently misinformation, of a malicious nature regarding an employee. Such "gossip" spreads quickly among the inmate population and, unfortunately, is sometimes perpetuated by other staff members. The rumor clinic is closely related to disreputation in that the goal of both ploys is to discredit an employee. However, in the rumor clinic, an inmate seeks to damage a staff member's reputation beyond repair because the inmate does not like the employee and wants to discredit the employee. There is often a kernel of truth to the rumor which, despite considerable distortion or exaggeration, enhances its plausibility.

****

An inmate in a maximum-security men's prison circulated a rumor that a female correctional officer assigned to his unit was having sex with a certain inmate after the midnight count. The rumor was of little interest to most inmates because the officer had a solid reputation throughout the institution. However, the inmate who initiated the rumor posted a "diary" on the unit's bulletin board. This handwritten note chronicled the alleged sexual encounters between the officer and the inmate. The note was confiscated by another staff member who turned it over to the shift supervisor.

An investigation ensued and it was determined that the officer had, in fact, been letting the inmate out of his cell night after night. However, it was also concluded she was not having sex with the inmate; rather, she was having him mop and wax the floors in the unit. The shift supervisor had previously complained about poor sanitation in the unit and the officer had hoped to improve her performance evaluation rating for the quarter. The correctional officer was reprimanded for breaching security and showing favoritism to an inmate. The inmate who originated the rumor later admitted that he knew that no sexual activity was occurring, but that he felt "jealous" of the attention the other inmate was receiving from the officer.

Revenge

Revenge refers to an effort by inmates to retaliate against a staff member because of perceived mistreatment or neglect. Revenge can assume many forms, but typically involves the allegation of abuse or another policy violation on the part of an employee. In most cases, the inmate is hurt or angry as a result of an action or inaction by a staff member and concocts some plan intended to make the employee suffer financially or emotionally. The retaliatory scheme usually entails filing a grievance or initiating a frivolous law suit. Other modes of retaliation behavior include vandalism, sabotage, or even theft.

* *

The first author vividly recalls being the target of an inmate's revenge following an unpleasant encounter several years ago. The inmate had been extremely disruptive during drug education classes and had frequently challenged the drug treatment specialist's authority. Based on the treatment specialist's recommendation, the author called the inmate to his office to issue a notice expelling the student from the class. The inmate remained silent during the brief meeting but exhibited an icy, malevolent stare that seemed to say, "You'll pay for this!" At the end of the day, the author could not locate his date book, which, among other things, contained addresses and phone numbers of family, friends, and colleagues. A subsequent shakedown of the inmate's cell resulted in the discovery of the date book's cover but not its contents. The author undertook the painstaking process of contacting everyone whose name was included in the date book and warning them that they might receive a threatening or obscene communication from the inmate.

Ingratiation

Ingratiation refers to a ploy whereby inmates endear themselves to a staff member by saying or doing something for which the employee feels a sense of gratitude and possibly the inclination to reciprocate. Common forms of ingratiation include complimenting an employee on his or her appearance, telling a counselor or psychologist how competent or helpful he or she is, and offering a gift to a "favorite" correctional officer. Such acts of endearment are performed by the inmate without asking—at least openly—for reciprocation. Ingratiation, therefore, differs from negotiation in which there is an explicit quid pro quo arrangement.

* *

Marshall (introduced in Chapter 3) was master of his domain as the sole inmate assigned to the "kosher kitchen" at a federal penitentiary. He always made a point to make note of the foods enjoyed by each shift lieutenant. He would then plan the daily menu in accordance with the lieutenants' work schedule. One of the lieutenants, who was a notorious "chow hound," routinely began his shift by going to the kosher kitchen and seeing what meal Marshall had prepared. One of the inmate's many "hustles" involved taking large quantities of food from the dining hall to his housing unit where he would give some to his friends and sell the rest to other inmates. Not once was Marshall ever stopped for a pat search upon exiting the dining hall, because the evening shift correctional officers "understood" that Marshall "took care" of the lieutenants and was, therefore, to be "left alone."

****

Loretta had already served nine years on a twelve-year sentence in a large women's prison. She made her "living" in prison by making stuffed animals for other offenders and their children. The high quality of her work was well known throughout the institution and she was kept busy with orders seven days a week. However, Loretta always made time to chat with housing unit staff and find out as much as she could about their children and other aspects of their personal lives. The offender noticed that a recently employed counselor decorated her office with bunny rabbit pictures and figurines. One morning she was surprised by Loretta who presented her with a magnificent stuffed rabbit. The counselor was momentarily speechless but finally said, "Loretta, I can't accept this. It's too nice. You should give it to one of your children." Loretta replied, "My children are grown. Besides, the bunny will look great in your office." The counselor reluctantly accepted the rabbit and profusely thanked Loretta for her thoughtfulness and commended her for her talent and effort.

Several weeks later, Loretta submitted a request for "outside clearance" to be able to do clean-up and minor repair work at state parks. Technically, she did not qualify for such work assignments because of the nature of her crime (second-degree murder). Nevertheless, the counselor processed the request and persuaded the classification supervisor to make an exception for Loretta.

Splitting

Splitting refers to a maneuver whereby an inmate pits one staff member against another to curry favor from or undermine the authority of one or both employees. This manifestation of the power orientation is a variation of the classic military strategy known as "divide and conquer." Typical methods of creating conflict or mistrust between staff members include: telling one employee that another has made a derisive remark about him or her; informing a correctional officer that a colleague has reversed a decision made by the former; or misrepresenting an employee's action to a supervisor such that the employee is overruled. In splitting, an employee becomes angry and may even enter into conflict with a fellow staff member while the inmate who created the tension sits back and waits to take sides. The inmate will align himself or herself with the staff member who has the most to offer.

****

A male substance abuse counselor working in a women's prison filled in for a colleague who was on maternity leave. The "substitute" enacted very stringent standards for homework assignments and class participation. The offenders enrolled in this class complained and rebelled throughout the four weeks their assigned clinician was on leave. Upon her return to work, the offenders told her that her "replacement" had made several sarcastic comments about her pregnancy and maternity leave. The clinician dismissed these allegations and opted to give her colleague the benefit of the doubt.

At the weekly staff meeting later in the week, the program coordinator asked the male clinician to describe his experience while filling in for his colleague. He reported that the offenders had been extremely uncooperative and resistant, and that he hoped that his fellow clinician "didn't plan on having any more kids for a long while." The female clinician became enraged and shouted, "You sexist bastard! Those ladies told me the truth about what you said about me." She then stormed out of the meeting and contacted an Equal Employment Opportunity counselor to discuss bringing sexual harassment charges against her colleague.

The following day the female clinician apologized to the offenders for not believing what they had said about her colleague's remarks. She also told them that they did not have to complete any unfinished homework that had been assigned during her absence. Moreover, she assured the offenders that her male colleague would not be asked to provide input into their quarterly progress reviews.

Boundary Intrusion

Boundary intrusion refers to an attempt by an inmate to establish a personal relationship with a staff member. The goal of this power thrust is to neutralize the employee's status as an authority figure and create a level "playing field" with the inmate. The erosion of the staff/inmate boundary can be subtle, such as calling one another by first names, or overt, such as mutual touching. In all cases, however, it becomes increasingly difficult for the employee to hold the inmate accountable for rule infractions, and the inmate gradually escalates requests for special favors. Moreover, other inmates often witness a boundary intrusion and expect to be accorded similar accommodations. In extreme cases, interpersonal boundaries become so blurred that the employee and offender enter into a business arrangement or sexual relationship.

* *

Thomas was assigned to work as a mechanic in the vehicle maintenance department at a minimum-security facility. He was pleased to discover that he and his foreman, Rick, had grown up in the same hometown. Almost immediately, the two men started calling each other by their first names, joking with one another, and talking at length about mutual acquaintances. The other inmates who worked in the "garage" resented the fact that they had to work while Thomas was able to "slack off." However, they did not complain because Thomas talked Rick into letting all the inmates go to lunch and stop working early each day.

About a month before Thomas was to be released from the "camp," he approached Rick with a business proposition: He suggested that the two jointly purchase an auto body shop in their hometown. Rick, who was still a few years away from retirement, agreed to cosign a bank loan to start the new business which would initially be operated by Thomas. Four weeks after Thomas had been released from prison and had received the loan money, he absconded from parole and may have left the country. Worse yet, since Rick was obliged to repay the loan, the bank contacted the camp administrator and requested that Rick's wages be garnished. This led to an investigation into possible misconduct and the discovery that Rick had entered into a business relationship with an inmate. Rick resigned his position, thereby forfeiting his retirement earnings, in lieu of being fired.

Sphere of Influence

Sphere of influence refers to an inmate's exploitation of political, financial, or other personal resources to undermine staff authority or circumvent established policy and procedure. Some inmates wield considerable power and influence over other offenders as a result of their position in the hierarchy of a prison gang or an organized crime group. Other prisoners exert considerable influence behind bars through the financial resources they have amassed during their criminal careers. Still others accrue substantial power and control through their reputation as physically dominant or violent. Another sphere of influence involved in the successful manipulation of staff derives from an inmate's direct or indirect connection to an important political figure.

****

Tyrone was notified that he had been expelled from a drug treatment program because of numerous complaints that he had threatened, intimidated, and even assaulted other program participants. On the basis of a technicality, he was found not guilty of an assault for which he had been charged. However, the drug program coordinator reaffirmed her decision to expel Tyrone based on anecdotal evidence available to her, as well as the unsatisfactory level of his participation in classes and groups. The inmate's appeal of this decision was denied at every step of the administrative remedy process.

Unbeknownst to the coordinator, Tyrone's aunt was engaged to be married to an aide to a congressman. The politician, at the aide's request, wrote a letter to the warden in which he expressed concern that Tyrone's "rights" had been violated since his expulsion had followed a "not guilty" finding by a disciplinary hearing officer. Even though agency policy granted the coordinator broad discretion in the selection and retention of program participants, the warden directed that Tyrone be readmitted to the program in the service of the "best interests of all concerned."

Solidarity

Solidarity refers to an organized attempt by a group of inmates to compel staff to undertake a course of action considered favorable or to abandon a planned initiative regarded as unfavorable. Solidarity is usually based on inmates' geographic origin, religious affiliation, gang memberships, racial or ethnic identity, and similar demographic factors. Ultimately, of course, there is a sense of solidarity which derives simply from the experience of being held captive; in other words, inmates subscribe to the notion that "we're all in this together." Consequences of solidarity include food and work strikes, dining hall or housing unit disturbances, and even hostage-taking situations. Such actions can become quite violent and dangerous to both inmates and staff. However, for the purposes of this book, the authors are concerned with solidarity-based "power plays," which are more limited in scope and less volatile in expression.

****

Several offenders participating in a culinary arts program at a women's prison registered a complaint with the supervisor of education upon learning that one of their fellow students would not be permitted to attend graduation ceremonies. The offender had burned herself while cooking and had been found guilty by a conduct adjustment board of failing to observe required safety standards. The supervisor rejected the offenders' complaint but informed them that the newly appointed commissioner of corrections would be attending the graduation ceremony and the meal afterwards. The meal, which was to consist of foods prepared by the graduates, was intended to showcase the effectiveness of the culinary arts program. The soon-to-be graduates of the program submitted a letter to the superintendent of the facility in which they vowed to leave the program and relinquish their diplomas as a gesture of support for their fellow student. The superintendent, anxious to avoid an embarrassing situation involving the commissioner, reversed the conduct adjustment board's decision and permitted the offender to graduate with her peers.

****

Note: The astute reader may question whether the above scenario is actually another example of extortion. Overlap between the two expressions of the power orientation certainly exists. However, in the case of solidarity, there is no explicit threat or demand. The offenders in the culinary arts class agreed to a "sacrifice" they were willing to make in support of their peer but, in so doing, induced the superintendent to reverse a position taken by his staff because of a "sacrifice" he was not willing to make.

Additional Illustrations

A brand new correctional officer was excited as she assumed her first duty assignment after completion of institutional familiarization training. She was assigned as a dormitory officer responsible for supervising seventy female offenders. Shortly after assuming her post, one of the offenders (Regina) approached the desk and asked the officer (Ms. Price) to call the maintenance department and advise them that one of the washing machines was not working. Meanwhile, another offender (Melanie) walked up to the desk, handed two Benadryl tablets to Regina, and remarked, "Here are the two "bennies" I owe you from last night." Ms. Price considered this interaction to be somewhat unusual, but determined that nothing must be wrong about it since it was transacted right in front of her.

Three weeks later, Ms. Price discovered that Melanie was wearing Regina's necklace. Since this was a clear violation of the rules prohibiting "loaning and borrowing," the officer informed Regina and Melanie that they would both be receiving disciplinary reports. The officer was not prepared for what happened next: Melanie positioned herself within inches of Ms. Price and loudly stated, "If you're smart, lady, you'd better tear those tickets (disciplinary reports) up, or else I'm gonna tell a white hat (supervisory officer) that you let us pass pills back and forth." Ms. Price appeared confused, so Melanie smugly reminded her of the Benadryl incident three weeks earlier.

Commentary: This vignette is an excellent illustration of two of the power and control maneuvers introduced at the start of this chapter. Notice that at the beginning of the incident, the officer was the victim of testing by Melanie, who passed the Benadryl tablets to Regina in an attempt to see if Ms. Price would react and, if so, what action she would take, if any. The astute reader might also argue that Regina's original approach was a diversion intended to confuse or defocus Ms. Price. Further, Melanie's forceful and indignant threat to inform a supervisor that Ms. Price had ignored an earlier policy violation was clearly an example of extortion.

****

A very high profile inmate had just arrived at the institution which would become his "home" for the remainder of his incarceration. One afternoon, the warden and associate warden were making rounds in the special housing unit where the inmate was housed, stopped at his cell, and asked him how he was doing so far. He responded, "I just don't know if I can do this time. I'm not sure it's worth it." The warden pulled the associate warden aside and instructed him to summon a psychologist to the unit at once. The psychologist, who had just finished responding to another inmate crisis, immediately reported to the special housing unit. Upon her arrival, the warden expressed his concern that the inmate might be suicidal.

The psychologist approached the inmate's cell and introduced herself. He was sitting on his bunk with his arms folded and appeared to be in no psychological distress whatsoever. Indeed, he was wearing a mischievous smile with a hint of arrogance. The psychologist inquired as to the meaning of the smile and the inmate replied: "You guys are pretty good. You got here seven minutes after I told the warden that I didn't know if I'd be around much longer. At my last joint it took fifteen minutes before a shrink showed up."

Commentary: In this scenario, one can readily see how the inmate experiences a sense of "duping delight" (Ekman, 1992) following his successful manipulation of staff. Correctional workers will find themselves the subjects of testing by inmates time and time again. Their reputation among the inmate population will be based in large part on whether they "pass" or "fail" these tests. New employees, in particular, can expect to face tests designed to determine their willingness and ability to establish behavioral limits and enforce rules and regulations.

****

Ronald was a rather dependent, inadequate inmate who was well known to the psychology department. Even though he lived in the least chaotic and dangerous housing unit in the institution, Ronald often requested temporary placement in administrative detention because of "stress" and "panic" which he attributed to the demands of day-to-day living in a maximum-security facility. Typically, after a few days of "rest" and "reflection," he would ask the officer in charge of the administrative detention unit to inform a psychologist that he was ready to return to the "compound."

One morning the chief psychologist received a call from the officer in charge who conveyed Ronald's message that he was ready to be released from administrative detention. The officer in charge, however, asked the psychologist to delay authorizing the inmate's release. According to the officer in charge, other inmates in administrative detention were reporting that Ronald was "selling" tobacco products (prohibited in administrative detention) to settle gambling debts he had incurred in the general population. The officer in charge indicated that he wanted to search Ronald's person and cell. The psychologist, who was quite distressed by this information, asked the officer in charge to notify him regarding the results of the search. An hour later, the officer in charge called the psychologist and informed him that officers had indeed found a large quantity of smoking materials hidden under Ronald's mattress. Moreover, the inmate had confessed that he had "muled" items to administrative detention every other time he had requested temporary placement.

Commentary: The chief psychologist in this scenario (the first author) was surprised and dismayed to learn of Ronald's deception, since the inmate had consistently displayed textbook symptoms of anxiety and depression. In fact, however, the psychologist was a victim of Ronald's skill at dissimulation; the apparent symptoms of a mood disorder were nothing but a diversion from his real agenda.

****

David Hilton-El was the recognized leader of one of the Islamic worship groups at the penitentiary where he was incarcerated. He was bright, articulate, and well versed in policies and procedures relevant to religious practices. One day, a recently employed chaplain entered the chapel's main congregation room where David and his "followers" were holding a worship service. As soon as the chaplain entered the room, David halted the service, walked toward the chaplain, and angrily exclaimed, "What in the name of Allah do you think you're doing by interrupting our service? Don't you know that you are in violation of RFRA (Religious Freedom and Restoration Act)? If you don't get out of here right now, I'll file a BP-9 (grievance) on you!"

The new chaplain, who feared that he had committed a major policy violation, immediately returned to his office and called the supervisory chaplain who was at home and reported the presumed indiscretion. The supervisor informed the chaplain that absolutely nothing in RFRA prohibited a staff member from attending or supervising any worship service. The supervisory chaplain also advised his subordinate that Hilton-El was well known throughout the prison system for undermining the authority of staff—especially chaplains—and transforming worship services into forums for the expression of antigovernment sentiment. The supervisor admonished the chaplain to never succumb to threats or intimidation from an inmate.

Commentary: This vignette is principally illustrative of the strategic use of extortion. However, the inmate also wields power and control attributable to his sphere of influence within the Islamic worship group. Moreover, Hilton-El successfully asserts power and control by testing the new chaplain's resolve. It is also feasible that the inmate accosted the chaplain to create a diversion from some nefarious activity in which he and his followers might have been engaged.

Sometimes extortion is more subtle in its expression. For example, the first author recalls asking an especially demanding and impatient inmate to wait until the next day to be seen. Fifteen minutes later, the author was called to the infirmary where the inmate was being treated for self-inflicted cuts to his wrists. The inmate smiled at the author and quietly asked, "Now, will you see me?" This is an excellent illustration of what Meunier, Lett, and Ethridge (1996) refer to as the "Suicide as a Means to an End" type of manipulative self-mutilation.

****

A male and female psychologist were walking through the main corridor of a men's prison after having made rounds in the special housing unit. They encountered an inmate who was an active participant in the drug abuse program. (The inmate had been confronted on several occasions by the drug treatment specialist for making statements that were demeaning toward women.) As the inmate approached the two psychologists, he greeted them in the following manner:

"Hello, **Dr**. Epstein (male psychologist)."
"Hello, **Miss** Bozarth (female psychologist)."

Commentary: This brief and seemingly innocent greeting is an example of disreputation. The inmate, who knows that both psychologists have identical degrees (Ph.Ds.), refers only to the male psychologist as "Dr." This was not an oversight; the inmate intentionally referred to the female psychologist as "Miss." He sought to diminish her status as a professional on equal standing with the male psychologist. The inmate very likely views women as second-class citizens and resents the fact that a woman is in a position to hold power over him. Therefore, he will devise a variety of strategies intended to diminish the authority and status of female employees to confirm his belief in his superiority to them.

Note: A variation of this strategy is to address a non-Ph.D. but male mental health professional as "Dr.," while addressing a female professional who has a Ph.D. as "Miss."

****

Drug Treatment Specialist:	"Today, we're going to discuss the effects of marijuana on the central nervous system."
Inmate:	"When's the last time you've been high, Mr. Gordon?"
Drug Treatment Specialist:	"I've never used marijuana."

Inmate:	"Then, how can you stand up there and preach to us about something you know nothing about?"

OR

Drug Treatment Specialist:	"Today, we're going to review the effects of marijuana on the nervous system."
Inmate:	"When's the last time you got high, Mr. Gordon?"
Drug Treatment Specialist:	"I tried pot in high school, but haven't used any drugs since."
Inmate:	"Then, you've got no business standing up there preaching to us. You're just a junkie like the rest of us!"

Commentary: Both of these staff/inmate transactions are examples of disreputation. In the first example, the specialist is discredited because he has no personal experience as a marijuana user. In the second interaction, his credibility is challenged for the opposite reason. In other words, the inmate has craftily manipulated Mr. Gordon into a "lose-lose" predicament. His authority and legitimacy will be discredited by responding in either manner to the inmate's question. Treatment staff—psychologists, teachers, counselors, and others—are discouraged from responding to such "set-ups." Instead, we recommend that they employ one of the "3 Rs" described in Chapter 8.

****

Johnny, a fifty-five year-old penitentiary inmate who had served most of his sentence for cocaine distribution, was informed by his case manager that he was eligible for a one-year sentence reduction if he successfully completed a drug treatment program. Shortly after his admission into a residential substance abuse program, he discovered that he did not like the dormitory-style unit in which the program was housed. Johnny much preferred the more secure "cell house" from which he had been reassigned. The inmate found himself in a dilemma: To complete the program and thus qualify for the year off his sentence, he had to live in the designated unit.

Johnny learned that his unit manager was looking for an orderly (janitor) to take care of the counseling complex. This was a job that received very little supervision and one for which only Johnny, by virtue of his longevity of incarceration, was eligible. He approached the unit manager with the following "offer:"

> "How ya doin', Boss? I know you need somebody you can count on to take care of the complex. We both know I'm your man. There's only one problem, though. I'll need to move to K block so I can be close to the Safety Department. You know how hard it is to get supplies if you're not right there on their doorstep. I can attend morning classes and take care of the complex in the afternoon. Do we have a deal?"

Commentary: This scenario serves as an example of a power and control maneuver best described as negotiation. The inmate, in effect, says to a staff member, "If you scratch my back, I'll scratch yours." Such offers of assistance always convey the outward appearance that the inmate is performing a favor for the staff member. In reality, however, the inmate is seeking to manipulate the employee into doing something that is outside the realm of standard practice or, worse yet, constitutes a violation of institutional policy. In this case, Johnny was asking his unit manager to make an exception to program guidelines requiring treatment participants to reside in a specific unit. If the unit manager agrees to this "deal," he will have established a precedent which may haunt him in the future.

****

Inmate:	"Hey, Mr. Peters (housing unit officer), I need to talk to you after lights out tonight."
Officer:	"Yeah, what's up?"
Inmate:	"I can't talk about it now. But something big's gonna go down this weekend."
Officer:	"If you've got something to tell me, then just go ahead and tell me. Otherwise, get back to your cell."
Inmate:	"I just don't want to see anybody in this unit get hurt, and I know you don't either."
Officer:	"Look, if you've got some information like that, you'd better give it up."
Inmate:	"If I do, what do I get in return?"
Officer:	"What do you want?"
Inmate:	"I need a couple of cartons of smokes."
Officer:	"I'll see what I can do."

Commentary: In this illustration of a negotiation, the inmate has achieved power over the officer by simply getting him to consider the request for cigarettes. The inmate has established the fact that now (or perhaps later) the staff member is amenable to reciprocal transactions. The authors are hesitant to condemn the practice of "rewarding" inmates for information, since the safety of staff and other inmates can be at stake. Nonetheless, it must be understood that such information comes with a price tag attached. In addition, the employee can count on being approached in the future by the same or other inmates who want to play "let's make a deal."

****

Frankie was well liked by staff and inmates alike. Staff members often let down their guard around him because he had served so much time in the institution that he was regarded more as a peer than an inmate. One day, Frankie walked by Counselor Jones' office and overheard him talking on the telephone with someone. The counselor was clearly in distress and sounded like he was crying. Frankie proceeded to knock on the door and enter the office. Mr. Jones appeared startled and embarrassed when he saw the inmate.

Frankie, pretending not to know that the counselor was on the phone, gestured as though to apologize for the intrusion and left the office. However, the inmate made sure not to shut the door completely.

Frankie stood outside the door and listened intently to the remainder of Mr. Jones' communication. It sounded as though the counselor was trying to explain to someone (a girlfriend?) why he had to terminate their relationship. Mr. Jones told the person that he'd been called to the warden's office that morning and asked to close the door behind him. The counselor stated that the warden told him that he had just received a call from Jones' wife who demanded that her husband bring an end to an affair that he was having with another employee.

Frankie assumed that Mr. Jones was carrying on with Miss Porter, a teacher, because he had frequently seen the two going out for lunch together. Frankie returned to his unit and told other inmates about what he had overheard, and asked them to "spread the word" throughout the compound. Within a matter of hours, the "affair" was widely reported and assumed to be true.

Commentary: In this vignette, Mr. Jones was the unfortunate victim of the rumor clinic, a power and control ploy intended to reduce the employee's status in the eyes of inmates or even other staff. It differs from disreputation, in which the inmate usually has an ulterior motive, or revenge, as illustrated in the next scenario. In the rumor clinic, the inmate's goal is primarily one of embarrassing the employee to experience a sense of triumph and excitement. Building oneself up by tearing others down is, after all, the essence of the power orientation (Walters, 1990).

****

Correctional officer Troy Stevens had recently married counselor Linda Biemick. Linda retained her maiden name but the marriage was no secret to inmates. Their shifts overlapped for a couple of hours each evening and Troy would come to work thirty minutes early and stop by Linda's office. For five straight days, Troy failed to appear at Linda's office at the usual time.

By the end of the week, the inmate mail runner, who always made a point to deliver Linda's mail when Troy was visiting her, spread the news that the couple had separated. On the following Monday, the rumor was exaggerated when Linda did not show up for work. The mail runner told other inmates that Troy had beaten her up over the weekend and he had been jailed. This rumor gathered even more momentum when Troy did not report for duty either. When Linda returned to work on Tuesday, after using a vacation day to visit her sister, she was besieged with words of sympathy from inmates who offered to "settle the score" with Troy.

On Wednesday, Linda and Troy, who had returned to work following a week of deer hunting, were called to the warden's office. The warden informed them that he had received a call from the Office of Internal Affairs which had been notified that Troy was physically abusing Linda. An Office of Internal Affairs investigator would be arriving the following week to interview Troy, Linda, other staff, and inmates. Troy was placed on "home duty" status until further notice.

It took the Office of Internal Affairs investigator only one day to determine that the allegation against Troy was completely false. Based on information from a confidential (inmate) informant, he learned that the mail runner had paid another inmate to have his wife make an anonymous call to the Office of Internal Affairs. A search of the inmate's cell revealed a diary in which he detailed his romantic and sexual fantasies about Linda. A recent entry indicated that his plan to "get rid of" Troy was moving "full speed ahead."

Although Troy was exonerated of the charges that he had engaged in domestic violence, he and Linda both suffered considerable embarrassment. The trauma of the investigation and the occasional off-hand remarks from both staff and inmates took their toll on the couple's relationship. Troy requested reassignment to the satellite camp facility and Linda moved in with her sister. The mail runner was disciplined and transferred to another facility where he bragged that he had "brought down" two staff members.

Commentary: These two employees were unfortunate victims of a vicious rumor that took on a life of its own. Correctional employees should be mindful that their behavior is under continuous surveillance by inmates. Any hint of interpersonal relationships or conflicts involving staff members are especially popular subjects for the rumor clinic. In Chapter 9, the authors discuss ways in which staff can protect themselves from destructive gossip and unwanted intrusion by inmates into their personal lives.

****

Charles was a depressed and rather dependent inmate who struggled to remain in the general population at a federal penitentiary. Because of his mental health problems and his difficulty adjusting to the prison environment, the chief psychologist succeeded in arranging the inmate's transfer to a special needs unit at a lower-security facility. Unfortunately, Charles was returned to the penitentiary after several months because he failed to complete even the minimal requirements of the special needs unit. Shortly after his return, he implored the chief psychologist to let him enroll in a residential values program. The program was housed in the smallest and safest unit in the institution. The psychologist agreed to do so, but reminded Charles that he would be expected to participate fully in program activities.

Approximately six weeks into the program, one of the program treatment specialists informed the chief psychologist that Charles was just not "cutting it" in the program. He was often late for class, seldom completed homework assignments, fell asleep during lectures, and refused to participate in group discussions. The psychologist presented Charles with a "last chance agreement" which stipulated that the inmate needed to "get with the program" or else face expulsion. Charles reluctantly signed the agreement, but within days it was obvious that he had no intention to comply with the agreement.

Accordingly, he was expelled from the program and placed in a less desirable housing unit.

Six months later, a graduation ceremony was conducted for the inmates who had completed the program. Halfway into the ceremony, the chief psychologist, who was master of ceremonies for the unit, was handed a message instructing him to immediately report to the prison infirmary. He arrived only to find Charles unconscious, the apparent victim of an overdose of his antidepressant medication. When Charles awoke, he smiled at the psychologist and asked, "How was the graduation ceremony?"

Commentary: This is a classic illustration of a revenge-based power and control maneuver. Charles deliberately selected the day of the graduation ceremony as the occasion for retaliation. In addition to inconveniencing the chief psychologist and interrupting the ceremony, Charles received an additional "payoff" for his effort. He was transferred to a medical center where he could live in a more comfortable, less "prisonlike" environment. Some readers might even wonder if the overdose was intended to "force" a transfer to a medical center. Indeed, it is entirely possible that extortion as well as revenge was involved in this example of the power orientation.

****

Theodore held staff in utter contempt and limited his interaction with them to that which was necessary to avoid disciplinary reports. His hatred toward staff was so obvious, however, that he had been charged with insolence three times. Most recently he had been found guilty of a safety violation in the factory where he worked. He blamed his superior for not having fully explained the safety features of the piece of equipment which he (inmate) had misused. Theodore swore to himself that the supervisor would "pay" for his negligence.

Several weeks later the institution was the recipient of an American Correctional Association (ACA) reaccreditation audit. It was widely known throughout the factory that tool control was a priority issue during the review. Theodore bribed another inmate to ask the supervisor for assistance with one of the machines. While the staff member bent over to inspect the machine, Theodore carefully removed two items from the supervisor's tool pouch and hid them behind another machine. At the end of the day, the supervisor was unable to reconcile his tools with the shadowboard and had to report the items as missing. This prompted an exhaustive search and proved to be a significant finding in the ACA audit.

Commentary: To Robert, like many inmates, revenge can be sweet indeed. One can only imagine the sense of satisfaction he experienced when the supervisor was reprimanded for his "failure to attend to basic safety and security procedures." This is an excellent illustration of a power thrust: the inmate successfully elevated himself from the depths of the zero state to a position of power and superiority. As discussed in Chapter 6, staff must constantly remain aware of the physical location of inmates, and pay close attention to offenders' nonverbal behavior as well as their own. (The astute reader will notice that diversion also contributed to this successful manipulation.)

****

Ricardo was a handsome, smooth-talking inmate who had completed nearly all of the educational and counseling programs available in the institution. He was currently enrolled in a residential drug treatment program, the completion of which virtually guaranteed a transfer to a lower-security prison closer to the inmate's home. Approximately three months after Ricardo's enrollment, a new psychologist took over the leadership of the program. She proved to be much more involved in classes and groups and demanded more from the inmates than her predecessor.

Ricardo had become accustomed to "floating" through treatment programs with little or no effort, and he resented the new coordinator's intrusion into his "comfort zone." One day, Ricardo asked Ms. Channing, a relatively new treatment specialist, if he could speak with her privately after group. (The inmate had made a habit of complimenting Ms. Channing on her wardrobe and frequently came to her rescue when other inmates in the group questioned her expertise or disagreed with something she said.) When Ms. Channing closed her office door and asked Ricardo to sit down, the inmate said:

> "You know, Ms. Channing, I've been talking with several of the guys and we all agree that Dr. Henry (the program coordinator) disrespects you the way she's always interrupting you whenever you try to make a point. I know she's your superior, but she still ought to let you teach the class. I mean, you've been doing a great job ever since I've come into the program and you've really helped me a lot. I just don't like the way Dr. Henry comes in and takes the class over from you. It's like she's afraid you're going to show her up or something."

Commentary: In this scenario, the inmate executes not one, but two different power and control maneuvers. Complimenting the treatment specialist on her appearance, defending her against criticism from other inmates, and lavishing her with praise are all examples of ingratiation. Ricardo's obvious attempt to drive a wedge between Ms. Channing and Dr. Henry is a textbook illustration of splitting. The specialist's best course of action in this situation is to employ the relabeling and reversal techniques discussed in Chapter 8.

****

Kenny was a freckle-faced, energetic fourteen-year-old who had been committed to the Department of Corrections following his conviction in juvenile court for a string of residential burglaries. He had lived in various group homes and residential treatment facilities, and was no stranger to incarceration. Indeed, his institutional behavior was exemplary and he rapidly progressed through the prison's behavior modification program. He had just been promoted to "honor" status and enjoyed his first weekend furlough with his family.

On the Monday following his return from the furlough, Kenny asked his counselor if there was any way that he could be considered for early release. The youth indicated that his parents had raised the issue over the weekend. They hoped to enroll him in a private school next year, but to do so, he would have to be released at least a month earlier than the date currently projected. The counselor replied that he doubted that an early release was possible, but agreed to discuss the matter with the assistant superintendent. Kenny thanked the counselor for his willingness to "go out on a limb" and remarked, "The only reason I've done so well in the program so far is because you've been there for me, Mr. Elliott."

On Wednesday, the counselor met with the assistant superintendent and made an impassioned plea in support of an early release for Kenny. The counselor's presentation was so convincing that the administrator, who was skeptical to say the least, reluctantly agreed to approve the request. The counselor gleefully informed Kenny that he would be released in time to enroll in the new school. The offender tearfully looked at the counselor and said, "You know, Mr. Elliott, I would have never ended up in a place like this if you'd been my dad."

The following Monday morning, the counselor was called to the assistant superintendent's office. The administrator wore a smug expression on his face and stated, "Bill, I thought you might like to know that the young man you went to bat for last week is now in SQ (secure quarters). He picked up a woman's purse at the movies over the weekend and rifled through it looking for cigarettes. One of the other kids snitched him out to staff because he wouldn't share any of the smokes." The counselor emerged from the administrator's office feeling confused and embarrassed, but mostly angry—at both Kenny and himself. He called the youth's adoptive parents to give them the bad news and made a startling discovery. They had no plans whatsoever to enroll Kenny in a private school and did not want him to come home until he had fully "learned his lesson."

Commentary: This vignette in which the youth shrewdly ingratiates himself with the counselor is drawn from early in the first author's career when he worked with incarcerated juvenile offenders. The experience with Kenny taught the author an important lesson which served him well over the next twenty-five years: One must adopt an attitude of "healthy skepticism" at all times when working with inmates. The critical importance of such a perspective and specific strategies for developing it are discussed in Chapter 9.

****

Jason Caldwell was a rather slow-moving, complacent correctional officer who was quite popular among the inmates because of his lax enforcement of rules. However, he was not held in high regard by fellow officers and received only mediocre performance evaluations from his supervisors. One evening he was approached by Anthony, an inmate whom Jason had known for several years. Anthony told Jason that some of the other officers were "fixin' to do him." Jason asked the inmate what he meant and Anthony replied, "Hey, man, there's talk that Overton and Ripley (two other correctional officers) are gonna set you up for a fall. If you don't believe me, just ask Cowboy (another inmate)."

Jason was furious. He didn't like the other two officers and knew that the feeling was mutual. He reasoned that they were more than capable of doing something to get him fired, or at least some "time on the street" (suspended). Jason was not about to let that happen. He decided to be proactive: He took Anthony aside and solicited his help in "getting them (Overton and Ripley) before they get me." Jason proposed that Anthony spread a rumor that the two officers had become intoxicated and were thrown out of a "strip club" while attending an out-of-town training session. Anthony smiled and said, "Don't worry, boss, I've got you covered."

A week later Jason was summoned to the lieutenant's office where Officers Overton and Ripley were seated. The lieutenant informed Jason that the two officers had lodged a complaint that he (Jason) had made false allegations against them. The supervisor further explained that an inmate, subsequently identified as Anthony, had told the two officers that Jason had asked him to spread a "vicious lie" about them. Jason was shocked and unable to speak. He finally told the lieutenant that he wanted to speak with a union representative.

Commentary: Jason clearly displayed conduct unbecoming of a professional correctional officer and was disciplined for his behavior. However, readers are asked to focus their attention on the actions of the inmate. Anthony engineered a masterful display of splitting. He literally pitted one officer against two others and created a highly volatile situation which he could view from the "sideline." One can only imagine the exhilaration Anthony experienced as he wielded power and control over three staff members.

****

Gregory was well established as a tutor in the education department. He was so highly regarded by the teaching staff that he was able to move throughout the department without supervision, was asked to run errands for the secretary, and most importantly to the inmate, allowed to use the copy machine. Gregory had another job, albeit an unauthorized one. He was one of the institution's most popular and successful "jailhouse lawyers." His job assignment as a tutor fed his ego, while his work on inmate legal briefs enabled him to purchase his favorite items from the commissary. Unfortunately for Gregory, he started to experience difficulty meeting his "client's" legal deadlines without greater access to the copy machine. The inmate desperately needed to find a way to use the machine during evenings and weekends.

Gregory, always one to keep close tabs on staff "gossip," learned that one of the teachers, Mrs. Andrews, had been served divorce papers by her husband who planned to marry his secretary. The teacher was, quite naturally, devastated by this development and was often tearful in her classroom. Gregory began at once to volunteer to do errands for Mrs. Andrews and compliment her on her appearance. Within a matter of days, he managed to convince the supervisor of education to allow him to be Mrs. Andrews' tutor. The teacher, unable to concentrate on her duties, became increasingly dependent on Gregory to "run" the classroom.

One afternoon, after all the other inmates were gone, Gregory told Mrs. Andrews that he had heard about the turmoil in her personal life and offered to "listen" any time she needed to talk. She immediately broke into tears and disclosed the sordid details of her pending divorce. Gregory listened with apparent interest and offered to make himself available for "support," day or night. Mrs. Andrews, whose children were grown and no longer at home, began staying at work later and later to share her thoughts and feelings with Gregory. She also opened up the copy machine room for him, often waiting hours for him to finish copying materials he needed to meet "deadlines."

Commentary: This is a sad but vivid illustration of a power and control strategy best described as a boundary intrusion. Gregory transcended the role of an inmate and actually became a friend and confidant to the teacher. Gregory, like many inmates, routinely raised his "antenna" to locate staff vulnerabilities. The teacher was eventually accused of becoming romantically involved with Gregory and was encouraged to resign her position. Guidelines for limiting self-disclosure and protecting interpersonal boundaries with inmates are discussed in Chapters 8 and 9, respectively.

* *

Fred Wilson was a well-experienced, highly respected correctional officer who was regularly assigned to work in one of the housing units in a women's prison. He was one of the few male officers against whom offenders had never made allegations of sexual impropriety. One of the women (Zoe) in the unit for which Fred was responsible had learned through the grapevine that the officer was about to become a grandfather. Zoe desperately wanted to be selected as a member of the offender council, an advisory group to the superintendent, and she needed a favorable recommendation from a housing unit officer in order to be considered. Therefore, she and two other offenders crocheted a sweater, cap, and booties for the new baby. When the women presented Fred with the gifts, they said in unison, "We love you, Mr. Wilson." Fred, who was deeply touched by the offenders' thoughtfulness and generosity, replied, "I love you, too, ladies."

A week later, Fred overheard an argument in one of the rooms down the hallway from his office. He arrived in time to see one offender, Carla, poised as if to strike another offender, Vanessa. Fred instructed Carla to face the wall, conducted a pat search of her clothing, handcuffed her, and escorted her to administrative detention. He proceeded to write a disciplinary report wherein he charged her with attempting to assault Vanessa. Several days later, Fred was summoned to the shift supervisor's office and was informed that Carla had made allegations that Fred was sexually harassing her. She claimed that he had touched her buttocks and breasts in a sexually aggressive manner while pat searching her.

Fred was exonerated because the incident had been witnessed by several other offenders, including Vanessa, who disputed Carla's claim. However, Carla also cited the time a week earlier when Fred had said, "I love you, too. . ." to other offenders. The other women confirmed that Fred had made a statement, but explained to the investigator that it was simply an expression of gratitude and affection—not a romantic or sexual innuendo. Fred, whose conduct record had been unblemished to date, was issued a letter of reprimand charging him with violations of two elements of the code of conduct: 1) accepting unauthorized items (gifts) from an offender, and 2) directing inappropriate language ("I love you") to an offender.

Commentary: Although this vignette is suggestive of revenge (on the part of Carla) and ingratiation (by Zoe), it is primarily illustrative of boundary intrusion by Zoe and her two friends, as well as poor boundary management by the correctional officer. The giving or receiving of gifts, as well as expression of affection or familiarity, transforms the staff-inmate relationship from one which is strictly professional to one which conveys the appearance of impropriety.

The careful management of interpersonal boundaries, (a topic discussed at length in Chapter 9) serves to protect staff and inmates from allegations of improper conduct.

****

John Swinford, a member of a white supremacist group, approached the warden one day and registered a complaint that Alcoholics Anonymous (AA) meetings were not offered to the inmate population. Swinford told the warden that such meetings were available in every other institution in which he had done time. The warden thanked the inmate for his input, but needed time to assess the general interest in AA throughout the institution. The next day, Swinford returned to the warden with several other inmates who expressed an interest in attending AA meetings. The warden asked the chief psychologist to meet with the inmates and begin offering AA meetings as soon as possible. The psychologist and a drug treatment specialist met with the inmates and it was decided that weekly meetings, under the supervision of the specialist, would commence in one week.

After observing several meetings, the specialist informed the chief psychologist that the inmates were spending very little time discussing alcohol abuse and recovery issues. Instead, they were complaining about harsh treatment by correctional officers and making derisive comments about black inmates. The counselor further noted that all inmate participants resided in the same housing unit. The chief psychologist directed the specialist to convert the meetings from the AA format to that of a generic 12-step recovery model, and to advertise the meetings throughout the institution.

Immediately after learning about the conversion, Swinford declared that he and his fellow "soldiers"would not tolerate such "blasphemy." He claimed that they were alcoholics—not drug addicts, compulsive gamblers, or whoever else might attend the secular meetings. He proceeded to storm out of the meeting room closely followed by the inmates. Within two weeks, Swinford managed to convince the prison chaplain to sponsor AA meetings for a select group of inmates.

Commentary: In this vignette, power and control was exercised throughout by group solidarity. Interestingly, Alcoholics Anonymous and similar meetings are popular forums for certain inmate groups (or gangs) to discuss how to cultivate power and influence within the prison. This is especially true when the meetings are conducted without staff supervision and monitoring. Inmates also use religious services, social organizations, and various programs sponsored by well-meaning but naive volunteers as opportunities to quench their thirst for power and control within the institution. Power-hungry inmates will even abuse their "authority" when they are placed on inmate advocacy committees or in leadership positions within so-called therapeutic communities. However, this ability to wield influence derives from their success at instilling a sense of solidarity among specific groups of inmates. (Readers should note that no one—including managers and the warden—is immune to inmates' expression of the power orientation.)

****

The chief of psychology services at a federal penitentiary was called to a meeting with the acting warden and several unit managers who were planning for a potential crowding problem. The psychologist suggested relocating twelve inmates from a quasimental health unit, with the capability of accommodating thirty-two inmates, to the unit which housed the residential drug abuse program where twelve cells were vacant. This recommendation was approved and the decision was made to move the twelve inmates immediately. The chief psychologist proceeded to meet with the drug treatment staff to assign the inmates to specific cells. It was decided that the twelve inmates should be housed together on the same range; unfortunately this would require the relocation of several inmates enrolled in the drug program to other ranges.

Once the arrangements had been made, including plans for the notification of affected inmates, the chief psychologist and the drug program coordinator left the institution for a late lunch. Within fifteen minutes, each received emergency pages from different drug treatment specialists who advised them that program inmates were "bucking" at the prospect of being relocated to different ranges and were threatening to leave the program. Some of the inmates had already approached administrative officials with requests to return to their former housing units. The two psychologists immediately returned to the institution to undertake "damage control."

The drug program coordinator met with the angry and resistant inmates in her program while the chief psychologist tried to calm the anxious and agitated "mental health" inmates who felt like unwanted intruders in their new unit. The drug program inmates vehemently objected to being dislocated by "a bunch of nuts" and threatened to file grievances regarding the "contamination" of their unit by inmates who were not program participants. The coordinator countered by suggesting that the inmates were behaving in a manner inconsistent with the values (tolerance and flexibility) emphasized in the program.

Unbeknownst to the psychologists, virtually all of the inmates in the drug program had signed a petition in which they threatened to terminate their involvement in the program. Moreover, they vowed to discourage inmates throughout the institution from enrolling in the program because they would "get jerked around." The acting warden, after consultation with the warden who was attending a conference, informed the chief psychologist that the "mental health" inmates were to be "distributed" throughout the unit and that no program participants were to be dislocated. Upon hearing about the warden's decision, several of the drug program inmates "high fived" one another and congratulated themselves on their "victory."

Commentary: This vignette, like the one before it, represents the exercise of the power orientation through group solidarity. The drug program inmates banded together to dissuade staff from implementing an initiative perceived by the former as unfavorable. Such overt resistance is seldom effective when employed by only one or two individuals. The astute reader will note how the coordinator confronted the drug program inmates regarding the discontinuity between their presumed desire to change and their rejection and condemnation of the mental health inmates.

****

Sergio had been a successful banker who was serving a five-year sentence for fraud and embezzlement. He had served in several civic organizations in his community and was very active in local politics. During an interview with his probation officer, who was compiling information for the presentence investigation report (PSI), Sergio denied any history of alcohol or drug abuse whatsoever. However, shortly after arrival at the federal prison camp where he was to serve his time, he learned that a sentence reduction of up to one year was possible for inmates who completed a residential substance abuse treatment program.

Approximately two weeks after he had completed the application to enroll in the residential treatment program, the program coordinator informed Sergio that he was ineligible for program participation because his preliminary sentence investigation reflected no history of substance abuse. The inmate promptly appealed the coordinator's decision and was overruled at every step of the administrative remedy process. Sergio then focused his efforts on obtaining documentation from external sources to support his contention that he had, in fact, been treated for alcohol abuse a few years earlier. The coordinator received a letter from a social worker which was rather vague regarding the nature and extent of treatment. Subsequent inquiry revealed that the social worker was a tenant in one of the buildings Sergio owned. Other letters were received from members of the clergy, physicians, and attorneys but they, too, lacked the necessary information to justify admission into the program.

Not one to admit defeat, Sergio convinced the camp administrator, over the objection of the drug treatment program coordinator, to allow an independent team of mental health professionals to evaluate him for evidence of psychological problems secondary to alcohol abuse. Not surprisingly, the psychologist and psychiatrist, who were paid by Sergio's attorney, found that the inmate did indeed meet the diagnostic criteria for alcohol abuse. The attorney also convinced the judge to order an amendment to the presentence investigation to reflect the team's findings. Consequently, six months after the original denial, Sergio was found eligible for program participation and transferred to another camp where the program was available.

Commentary: This example of power and control is exemplified by the inmate's strategic use of his sphere of influence. In Sergio's case, his influence owed to his wealth and access to external resources. Other factors that enhance an inmate's sphere of influence include a reputation as a violent predator, notoriety of criminal history, and occupation of a leadership position in an organized crime "family," drug cartel, or notorious gang.

****

Fred (a.k.a. "Doc") Myers was a legendary inmate known throughout the entire prison system for his skill at helping other inmates receive favorable dispositions at parole and clemency hearings. He was a certified public accountant who was serving a lengthy sentence for fraud and embezzlement, crimes which had forced several of his clients into bankruptcy. Fred was bright, charming, and a gifted writer who could put together a parole board "package" that made even the most recalcitrant inmate appear repentant and rehabilitated. He had been nicknamed "Doc" because he had earned a doctoral degree through correspondence courses at the University of South Africa.

One day Fred overheard a brand new correctional officer complaining that he had been inadequately trained to "run" a housing unit. Fred approached the officer, introduced himself, and said, "Don't worry about anything, Boss. Just tell me what you want done and I'll make it happen. The guys in this block listen to me." The officer was skeptical, but frustrated enough to accept the inmate's offer of assistance. The officer told Fred that he had recently taken a lot of "heat" from the shift lieutenant because of poor sanitation in the unit. Fred responded, "Give me one week, Boss, and I'll have this unit looking shipshape for you." Indeed, the unit scored highest on the very next housing unit inspection. The officer was commended by the lieutenant for the improvement and told to, "Keep up the good work." The officer thanked Fred for his assistance to which he replied, "Don't mention it, Boss. That's what I'm here for."

As the weeks passed, the officer relied more and more on Fred for his help in securing cooperation from the inmates in the unit. However, the officer was unaware that all of his communication with the inmates in his unit was being transmitted through Fred. Even more disturbing was the fact that the officer had no idea what was going on in the unit since he depended on Fred for all of his information. Some of the more experienced officers who worked on the officer's shift urged him to distance himself from Fred, warning that before long the inmate would be running the unit if he were not already. The officer thanked his colleagues for their input, but emphasized that the lieutenant was pleased with the way the unit was operating. The officer quipped, "If the Lieutenant's happy, I'm happy."

Several weeks later, a surprise shakedown was conducted in the housing unit. Several weapons and large quantities of alcohol and drugs were discovered. The other officers assigned to the unit were all reprimanded for their failure to "stay on top" of what was going on in their unit. The first-year officer, however, was terminated because he did not yet have permanent status. On his last day of employment, he approached Fred and asked, "Why didn't you tell me about all that stuff that the guys were warehousing?" Fred smiled and replied, "Because you never asked me."

Commentary: In this scenario, in which an employee lost his job, the inmate manifested the power orientation through his sphere of influence among other inmates in the housing unit. "Doc's" influence was attributed to his ability to provide a service—preparing parole board "packages"—which was highly valued within the prison community. The inmates would be more than willing to cooperate with Fred to remain on his "good side." Fred's selection of the rookie officer as the object of this manipulation was based on the staff member's disclosure that he was unprepared for his job. Discussing one's unhappiness, whether at home or on the job, in front of inmates is an invitation for exploitation.

PART III:
The "Gender" Strategies

Chapter 5

The Woman Offender and Gender-based Games

Even though women still make up only 6 percent of the prison population, the rate of incarceration increased faster for women (12 percent) than for men (8.5 percent) from 1980 to 1995 (Pollock, 1998). With this growth in the sheer numbers of women coming into contact with the criminal justice system, it is increasingly likely that you will be working with women offenders at some point in your career. To understand current criminal justice approaches to women criminals, it is important to review the history of correctional philosophy toward women.

The history of women's prisons reveals an evolution of attitudes toward women that mirrors the evolution of attitudes in free society. Women's prisons of the 1930s and 1940s were built according to a cottage plan, with separate small housing units that had kitchens and a much "softer appearance" (Pollock, 1998). Windows had draperies and floors were covered with rugs. Contrast this with prisons such as Alcatraz and other fort-like penitentiaries for men during the same period. Women's prisons were built to shield and protect women from men, so they were managed by women wardens and superintendents and run by women staff. The goal of corrections was to teach the incarcerated woman to act like a "lady" (Pollock, 1998).

Some of these attitudes toward women offenders persist today although more and more prisons offer sound vocational training programs and athletic activities to women during incarceration. It is important to understand how this context in which women offenders live contributes to the type of deception and manipulation they attempt to use. Offenders can be highly adaptive to their surroundings and will use the staff's beliefs about their "nature" against them. For example, if a staff member rigidly believes that all women offenders are weak and vulnerable, the offender will play the role and manipulate the staff to jump through all kinds of hoops for her. It is always important for staff to objectively view the strengths and weaknesses of the offender rather than to stereotype them or their situation.

The basic elements of con games are the same, regardless of the gender of the criminal, although some game maneuvers are more consistent with American cultural expectations for men and women. Women in our culture generally are considered to be the following things: emotional; sensitive; interested in relationships; interested in being good parents (and wives and sisters and daughters); and victimized by men. Thus, women offenders who want to deceive and manipulate staff often use these expectations as mechanisms to advance their con games. Women offenders often try to use psychological tools and positions, such as "tears," "learned helplessness," and the "victim stance" to maneuver staff and further their own criminal attitudes and behaviors.

Tears

Women offenders are far more likely than male offenders to use tears as a tool to manipulate staff. Male criminals have a sense that using tears is likely to cause staff to reject and disregard them. Using tears makes the offender seem weak and staff have a tendency to create the same expectancy inside the prison that is found in the greater free society: Men don't cry.

Male offenders know that tears are not likely to produce the effect they want in staff, especially male staff, and therefore they almost never use tears to perpetuate a mind game to con or manipulate staff. Women offenders, however, use tears as powerful tools to aid them in their maneuvers to manipulate and deceive staff. While tears can certainly be real expressions of frustration and sadness, it is important to realize that women offenders will also use tears as a first maneuver to set up staff for a con game.

The woman offender may use tears to appear remorseful in court or in any situation in which she wants to moderate the consequences. Women offenders often use tears more with male staff than with women staff, who may recognize them more readily as manipulative. It is wise to be cautious when the female offender begins to cry without any apparent provocation, or in a situation where she believes she has something to gain from the person witnessing the tears.

Learned Helplessness

When women offenders are intent on manipulating and deceiving staff, they often choose to maneuver male staff who seem vulnerable. Often offender "perceive" younger staff as being more naive and, therefore, more easily manipulated. Women offenders also target male staff who demonstrate a "paternalistic" attitude toward women, in other words, view women as the "weaker" sex who need men to take care of them. This stance is a tempting overture to women offenders who want to cash in on this sympathetic attitude. They know that by "playing" weak and helpless, they will make the male staff feel strong. Where we have seen in earlier chapters that male offenders use ingratiation to wedge their way into manipulating staff by doing things for them, women offenders ingratiate themselves with male staff by allowing the male staff to do things for them. By "acting" weak and helpless, the woman offender "allows" the male staff to play out their paternalistic role of caretaker and protector. Thus, the male is psychologically confirmed in the male role he believes he is expected to assume and the women offender enjoys the special attention and favors she has gained.

Here is an example of an offender using a male staff member's "paternalistic" attitude to her advantage.

Mary: "Mr. Smith, do you think you could help me move the ladders from the mop room? I can hardly budge them and I'm supposed to clean the room today."

Mr. Smith: "Sure, Mary. Those ladders were around when we had male inmates in this unit. They are too heavy for you girls!"

Mary: "Mr. Smith, you are the best! You are the favorite counselor on this unit! We all think you help us out more than any other person!"

Mary has been able to manipulate Mr. Smith into doing her work. In this scenario, Mary was able to get Mr. Smith to move all of the ladders out of the room for her and to fill the buckets she needed with water and carry them to her work area. Mary could hardly wait to tell the other inmates about what a "soft touch" Mr. Smith was. Mary felt especially powerful, because she had been given the job of cleaning out the mop room for "extra duty" as a consequence for a disciplinary report.

Mary had guessed correctly that Mr. Smith would have different standards for interacting with male and female offenders. Over time, she had watched him interact with the male staff and female staff. When the male associate warden came into the unit, Mr. Smith responded like he was in the military. He would snap to attention, maintain straight posture, and respond with "Yes, Sir" and "No, Sir" to questions. When the woman associate warden came into the unit, his demeanor was much different. Mr. Smith would smile, ask her if she would like a cup of coffee, and he would offer her his seat while he showed her the unit project on which he was working. Mary had no idea why Mr. Smith treated these two people of equal stature differently, but she was sure she could take advantage of it.

Also note that in this scenario, Mary found a way to flatter Mr. Smith based on what she has observed him to value. First, she senses he likes to feel "manly" and he feels this way when he "takes care" of women. Secondly, Mr. Smith's job title is a "counselor" and what better way to flatter a counselor than to tell him that he is the best helper? Mr. Smith might reframe how he views his job. Rather than being there to help Mary, he is there to help her learn to handle her life independently and to ask for assistance only when she needs it, not when she wants it.

Another aspect of this scenario which is important is that Mr. Smith inadvertently sabotaged the disciplinary process and the unit officer's attempt to correct Mary's irresponsible behavior of being out of bounds in the recreation area last week. The officer had written a disciplinary report, and as a consequence, Mary had been assigned extra duty hours and the task of cleaning the mop room. When Mr. Smith stepped in at Mary's request, he started doing the work for her and minimizing the impact of the consequence on Mary. When Mary has a chance, she will undoubtedly make the officer aware that Mr. Smith did her extra duty for her. This will probably lead to the officer confronting Mr. Smith and Mary will have been successful in splitting staff. She will perversely enjoy the feeling of revenge on the unit officer for writing a disciplinary report on her.

Mr. Smith and Mary would had been better served if he had told Mary that he had confidence in her ability to move the ladders or to figure out a way to clean around the ladders that did not involve him. This way, Mr. Smith would have avoided Mary's manipulation, countered her criminal conning, and maintained the integrity of the disciplinary process.

The Victim Stance

Much attention has been focused on the "abuse histories" of women offenders. Indeed, the number of women in prisons who have been physically, sexually, and emotionally abused is high. However, the number of women who have been abused is high in prosocial women as well. The number of men who have histories of abuse is high in male prisons, but there is almost no attention brought to these facts. To the extent people will grant offenders an "excuse" for their criminal behavior, the offenders will take it and use it. The "abuse victim's stance" is found more often among women offenders than men because it is not as culturally acceptable for men to talk about this, especially in groups. Staff should be cautious to not allow the "victim stance" to become a spot on which the offender can rest. Rather, it should be the point from which they start on the road to creating a responsible, prosocial life.

Women offenders find that they can use a history of "victimization" to manipulate staff to gain favors and special consideration and as an excuse for their criminal behavior. One staff member who worked with women offenders revealed to the second author that she had been sexually abused by her stepfather when she was an adolescent. This abuse occurred decades before society had accepted the reality of child sexual abuse and began to provide protections for children. She confessed that at the time, she felt she wanted to kill him, but she did not. She found her way out of the situation. She worked hard, went to college, and became a nurse. The coworker said that when women complained to her that they were abused and, therefore, had no choice except to become an addict and or a criminal, she would tell them her story. She said that usually put an end to using their past as an excuse for their current behavior. She was a role model for these women. She was sympathetic and supportive, but she also held them accountable for their criminal thinking and behaving. She did not allow them to use their past to manipulate her into granting special favors.

Gender-specific Maneuvers

In correctional populations, there are considerably more male offenders than women offenders; however, criminal patterns of thinking and the use of con games exist in both groups. We think it is important to provide information on gender-specific maneuvers because these are often overlooked in general training classes.

Having an understanding of how women offenders will put the "gender spin" on sentimentality and mollification when trying to manipulate and deceive will help you enormously to counter the first moves. Remember, the goal is to create a WIN-WIN situation for you and the women offenders. Helping her become a good person, instead of just perpetrating the myth that she is good, is your goal for her. Helping her understand that the past is history and is not an excuse for her current criminal thinking and behaving is also an appropriate correctional treatment goal.

Chapter 6

Games Women Offenders Play Based on Blaming or Mollification

"I may be locked up for victimizing others, but I am the real victim here."

In Chapter 2, we described mollification as the act of transferring blame onto something external. Many women offenders avoid taking responsibility for their criminal behavior by blaming their boy-friends (husbands) for leading them into criminal activity. This "vision of coercion" fits neatly into the mental images the media has created. There are a dearth of movies in which the dominant role in a criminal plot is played out by a woman. The media perpetuates the "woman as victim" who does what she does because she loves her man. She is not really bad, she just hangs out (and enjoys the ill-gotten gains) with someone who is bad. Let us examine this behavior more closely.

Andrews and Bonta (1998) identified characteristics that are unique and commonly found in criminals. They found that individuals who have "criminogenic needs" are at greater risk for future criminal behavior. One of these criminogenic needs is related to hanging out with others who are criminal. Very simply stated, criminals seek out other criminals and noncriminals seek out noncriminals. Increased procriminal associations increases the risk for recidivism (Andrews and Bonta, 1998). So, the woman prisoner who is trying to convince us that she is not a criminal (only her boyfriend is) is using mollification and blaming to mitigate her culpability.

What is really going on here? If you were introduced to some new people and then found out they were actively involved in selling cocaine, would you deliberately develop a relationship with those persons or would you decide you should distance yourself from them because of their criminal activity? Only criminals develop relationships with other criminals. Even if the woman does not think up the criminal activities, if she knows about them, she is criminally culpable. When the woman criminal blames the male criminal for her plight of being in prison, she is failing to take the first step in her own rehabilitation, accepting that she was responsible for her behavior.

"I'm not a drug dealer. I didn't think Jeff was selling drugs. He never told me that was what he was doing. How was I supposed to know?"

Marsha was new to the group on the unit and meekly began to tell her story. She and Jeff had been together for three years. They lived together but were not married. She worked periodically as a waitress and wanted to go to college, but just had not found the time. She met Jeff at a club when she was eighteen and he was twenty-five. Jeff told her he had been in jail before for something he didn't do. She told the group that she believed him. They smoked marijuana together and partied with friends almost every night. Jeff did not have a job and never looked for work. The year before they were arrested, they bought a new motorcycle and traveled around Canada for two months. Marsha said it was great.

Marsha said she could not believe it when the cops came to the house and arrested them. She later found out that there was a lot of cash, marijuana, and some cocaine in the house. She could not believe that the cops were holding her, too. What did she do? She said the only reason she was doing any time was that she would not tell on any of their friends. Her only crime was that she loved Jeff. She wants to marry him when they both get out of jail. Marsha said she just hopes the cops will leave them alone.

Commentary: In this example, Marsha is using mollification and is blaming everyone for her current plight. She makes excuses for not knowing that Jeff was engaging in drug deals, even though he did not work at a legitimate job and always had money for them to "party" and go on vacations. Marsha is trying to look like an "innocent" criminal. She even seems to want our sympathy. We can safely assume that Marsha had a very good idea that Jeff and his friends were drug dealers and that she fully enjoyed the fruits of his "criminal" labors. Marsha even "blames" the police for locking up Jeff and her and avoids accepting any responsibility for her behavior.

The reality is Marsha and her boyfriend were the main source of drugs for young kids in their town. She takes no responsibility for her role in victimizing young people by supplying them with illegal drugs. She only wants to complain how she has been victimized and treated unfairly by the system. If Jeff and Marsha had been working and not selling drugs, then the police would not have found any illegal drugs in their home. It is Marsha's behavior that led to her arrest.

Countermoves. The con game began with Marsha blaming others and making excuses for her current predicament. What is the best countermove you can make as a staff person to shut down her con game and help her take responsibility for her situation? Sometimes, the best countermove is the opposite of the initial con maneuver. Marsha's first move is to blame, then the staff's countermove is to throw the responsibility onto Marsha and have her accept it. Begin with getting her to accept responsibility for small parts of the scenario.

Staff: "Marsha, was it your decision to go out with Jeff when he first asked you? Marsha, was it your decision to move in with Jeff? Marsha, was it your choice to . . .?"

Slowly, Marsha begins to admit to her role in the criminal activity and that she alone is responsible for her situation.

Women offenders often blame their significant others for "making" them engage in criminal behavior. Staff have an important role in countering the offender's mollification. Because there are established patterns of criminal thinking, staff have a big job to do in reversing these patterns and modeling thinking patterns that are honest and lead to noncriminal behavior.

"I was sexually abused by my father when I was seven and later by my stepfather. I ran away and started using drugs and alcohol. I didn't care about anything or anyone. Why should I? No one ever cared about me. Yeah, I sold drugs. I had to support my habit. That's why I'm here."

Ericka's story was true. The sexual abuse by her father and step-father was documented in court records. Sexual abuse is devastating and profoundly affects the victim, sometimes for many years. Many adults who seek therapy for serious emotional problems have histories of sexual or physical abuse. Many women who abuse drugs and alcohol have abuse histories. Ericka spent years in and out of drug treatment programs and in and out of jails and prisons.

She always began treatment by telling the story of her abuse. She liked that she was able to provide the explanation for her drug taking and selling behavior. By telling the abuse story, she could keep the "therapeutic" heat away. Therapists never questioned her too much after they heard her story. Ericka thought, "How nice that they have been trained to be sympathetic to victims. It makes being in these damn groups much easier."

Commentary: This type of manipulation is particularly difficult for new criminal justice staff who work with women offenders. After all, here is a real victim. That Ericka is a victim of child sexual abuse is indisputable. It is no wonder she turned to drugs and alcohol. It would be almost intolerable to have the devastating memories of sexual abuse in one's consciousness.

Because Ericka is a victim, is she not justified in blaming the sexual abuse for her criminal behavior? Is this mollification when criminals really can blame someone or something for their behavior? Should we not show her sympathy?

Ericka's situation is a good example of beginning with the straight facts and then using faulty logic to arrive at an erroneous conclusion and criminal attitudes. Ericka's logic is that because she was abused, it was okay for her to become a drug addict and drug dealer. She believes that her abuse justifies her victimizing others by selling drugs to them. But this is indeed faulty logic. Let us start over. It is a fact that Ericka was sexually abused. However, does everyone who is sexually abused then abuse drugs? No. Does everyone who is sexually abused become a drug dealer? No. Does everyone who is sexually abused become a repeat criminal offender? No. So, Ericka's logic is faulty. By concluding that her drug addiction and repeated criminal behavior were caused by the sexual abuse, she has denied her own power over her life as well as her responsibility for her behavior. But why does she do this? By blaming her behavior on something outside of herself, she can avoid working on changing. This is cognitive indolence or psychological laziness, another type of criminal thinking pattern.

Ericka has taken a the "victim stance." She wants to keep thinking of herself as a victim and avoid thinking about the people she has "victimized" by selling illegal drugs. By keeping her focus and the focus of others on her victimization, she gains sympathy and avoids being held accountable for her criminal behavior. She has been "rewarded" for portraying herself as a victim in other drug treatment programs where she was "let off the hook" because of her past. She found she could shock well-intentioned therapists with graphic descriptions of the abuse. Using strong emotionality to chronicle the events, she could use up the group time and the therapists always felt like she had made "progress" because she was able to talk about the abuse. Ericka found that she was usually able to get special privileges and favors for at least a month after one of her performances in group.

This type of deception and manipulation is found in treatment groups and programs that fail to understand the relationship between the offender's past and the offender's current needs. While it is always important to understand the events of the past, that is not where the focus should stay. Especially with individuals who are criminal, those who work with them must appreciate the need for support and accountability. It is important to feel sympathy for Ericka and it is important to hold her accountable for her criminal thinking and behavior. As this example demonstrates, only showing sympathy and excusing her behavior reinforces it. And this is exactly the opposite of what we want to achieve with criminals.

Najavits (2002) notes that posttraumatic stress disorder (PTSD) tends to evoke sympathy from the therapist, "which if taken too far may lead to excessive support and overindulgence." On the other hand, behaving like a criminal (being irresponsible, manipulative and deceptive) can create negative feelings in the counselor, which may lead to "harsh judgment and confrontation" (Najavits, 2002). What we need to do is to achieve a balance of "praise and accountability, which are . . . the two central processes of treatment" (Najavits, 2002).

Countermoves. The first moves in this game began with Ericka "throwing out the bait" in the group therapy session. The "bait" was her story of being sexually abused. She was surely watching to see how staff would respond to her and hoping to see staff sitting on the edge of their seats with concerned facial expressions. The "countermove" has to begin with a nonverbal message to Ericka that communicates "I'm listening and I'm listening for you to make honest statements that indicate you accept that you are responsible for your criminal behavior that brought you here to prison."

When Ericka did not indicate that she believes she is responsible for her behavior or that her behavior was wrong and she needs to change, staff moves to let her know that these are the goals for her. The staff member can let Ericka finish the story and then plant the expectation that her future depends on her accepting the reality that her behavior is not controlled by her past, but is controlled by the choices she makes today. Keeping the focus on Ericka's current behavior, attitudes, and thinking patterns will help her do the same.

Chapter 7

Games Women Offenders Play To Look Good or Sentimentality

"I may be locked up, but I'm still a good mother."

When women offenders engage in con games, they often favor using the criminal behavior pattern of sentimentality to deceive and manipulate staff (Walters, Elliott, and Miscoll,1998). Sentimentality is deliberately trying to look like a good person and play on the good feelings of others to gain advantage and manipulate the staff or the system. Male offenders usually strive to seem "bad" when they are in prison so other offenders do not try to prey on them. Typically, women offenders do not worry as much about physical threats. The culture of a women's prison is not as tense as that found in men's prisons. This fact tends to support behaviors in women that are considered "good" in our culture. Women offenders will try to take full advantage of staff's expectations that they are "good." Once the offender senses which "good" behaviors are valued by the staff, she will try to "act" these behaviors.

Women who are caught up in the criminal justice system and have children will try to create an impression of being a "good mother" even though they commit crimes, use illegal drugs, and neglect the needs of their children. In the American culture, being a mother almost always assumes a "good" mother. It is hard for people who are caring and loving to imagine that a mother can be bad. We have strong protection under the law for parental rights because in our culture, parents are assumed to be the best people to take care of their children. There must be indisputable proof of neglect and abuse before a court will terminate parental rights. Women offenders find that using claims of being a good mother can often get them special attention and privileges.

"I have three kids out there. I need to be with them, not locked up in here. They need me. I just have to get home so I can take care of them."

Mary was a thirty-year-old offender who was serving three years for writing fraudulent checks. Her criminal history began in her early twenties and she had previous convictions for theft and fraud. When Mary was in jail or prison, she would take advantage of education and vocational programs. She had earned college credits and was familiar with several computer programs used in office work. Every time Mary was arrested, she managed to become pregnant in time for her eventual trial and sentencing. Mary believed that judges tended to be lenient with offenders who had young children and even more so with pregnant offenders. Playing the "sympathy" card seemed to work for her whenever she was caught up in the criminal justice system.

Mary's three children were nine, six, and four. She was currently five months pregnant. She managed to keep the children out of foster care because her mother would step in to help whenever needed. The children were often at their grandmother's house anyway, because Mary liked to go out to clubs. This would often begin a three-to-five-day hiatus from home and work. Mary's work history was sporadic. Although she had decent training and good skills, Mary's poor attitude about work led to marginal performance and chronic absenteeism.

Mary believed she was a good con. She had manipulated her mother for years into taking care of her and taking on her responsibilities. Her parents had divorced when Mary was seven, and her mother turned her full attention to taking care of Mary. Early on, Mary realized she could get anything she wanted from her mother by playing on her sentiments of guilt and the erroneous belief that giving your children everything they want makes you a good parent. Mary could also con her way into almost any job she wanted. She told the interviewers exactly what they wanted to hear and landed new jobs with ease. After a few months, the employers would realize that Mary was unreliable and unmotivated. She would begin lying and stealing and eventually resign or get fired. Mary was proud that there were only a couple of times she could not talk her way out of having the employer file charges against her.

Once in jail or prison, Mary's con games continued with staff. She would take care of others (when in clear view of staff) and spend time on the phone with her children. She wrote them letters that she would read to staff, and knitted them mittens and scarfs in hobby shop. Mary constantly begged staff to let her have extra visits and furlough privileges sooner than was normally granted. Mary was elated that she would get into a community placement because of her pregnancy. It sure beat being in prison!

Commentary: Mary lived her life using con games. She used them on her mother, her employers, criminal justice workers, other offenders, and even her children. She used deception and manipulated people to further her irresponsible antisocial lifestyle. By going through the motions of being a good mother and helping others, she manipulated the good sentiments of others. Those who see the surface behaviors and fail to look at the "whole" picture will surely be deceived. Mary has honed the skill of "looking good" at a superficial level and her deceptive ploys are intended to reel in those who do not know her well.

She deliberately omitted information that would cast her in a negative light. She has learned the skill of using "her children" and the fact that she is "a mother" as protection against some of the restrictions imposed by the criminal justice system and as a way of getting special consideration and privileges. The problem here is as much the fault of criminal justice policies as it is Mary's. Policies that grant special privileges because of parental status should be balanced by holding the offenders accountable for their criminal behavior and attitudes. The criminal justice system "rewarded" Mary for becoming pregnant by cutting her a break at sentencing and placing her in a community setting. This can be a good program, but it must also include groups and therapy to address Mary's criminal thinking.

The central problem with Mary is her criminal thinking patterns. She has a solid home and a parent who loves her. She is educated and has been trained in skills that can get her a job that will earn sufficient income for her and her children. The problem that has not been addressed by the criminal justice system is that her criminal attitudes have not been challenged. When we educate a criminal, we have an educated criminal! Unless we address the underlying criminality of offenders, the offenders will probably not change and we will see them again and again.

Countermoves. This is a situation that can easily end up as a WIN-WIN-WIN. If the countermoves are successful in shutting down Mary's con games, we win, Mary wins, and her children win. The best countermoves against Mary's con games are to hold her accountable for her behavior and reveal her underlying motives to her and others. Correcting her references to being a good mother to being a mother who wants to become a good mother is a start. Letting Mary know that you are aware of her manipulative moves but only intend to respond to her honest and prosocial behavior is a good countermove and strategy. It would be therapeutic for Mary to "own up" to her behavior in groups or with others in the unit and let them know that she has done things for them just so she could look good and get special privileges. Eventually, Mary should own her deception and manipulation to others such as her mother, her judge, her past employers, and her children. A word of caution: even these "honest" confessions can be manipulative, but at least they let others know what she has been doing to them. As the saying goes, the proof is in the pudding. With someone like Mary, we will not know if she has really changed until she is released from custody. If she then lives a responsible life and becomes a good mother, then she was not deceiving us about her changes. We can only do our best to show her the way to winning at life. It is up to her to do it.

Part IV:
It's Your Move: Staff Counter Plays

Chapter 8

Staff Moves in Managing Inmate Deception and Manipulation

By now, it should be readily apparent that manipulation is an integral part of inmate-staff interaction in a prison environment. We hope that Chapters 3 through 7 have equipped the reader with an appreciation for the myriad ways in which inmates lie, con, and otherwise attempt to deceive staff members. However, simply knowing that they are being conned does not enable the employees to handle the manipulative inmate successfully; they must effectively manage the situation to fully avoid further exploitation. Bud Allen and Diane Bonta (1981) and Boyd Sharp (2000) have listed some "protectors" and "survival skills," respectively, whereby correctional employees can prevent and/or minimize the harmful consequences of inmate manipulation. In this chapter and the next one, the present authors expand on these earlier contributions and identify a wide array of strategies which staff members can effectively use to guard against or at least manage inmate deception and manipulation.

The prudent staff member will assume that the potential for manipulation exists in almost every interaction with an inmate, and place the "burden of proof" on the offender to prove that he or she is being honest. That is not to say that prison staff should assume a paranoid or cynical stance toward inmates. Rather, we recommend that they subscribe to what Samenow (1984) refers to as an attitude of "healthy skepticism." (This notion is discussed in much greater detail in Chapter 9.) Just as important as anticipating and recognizing inmate manipulation is responding to its discovery promptly and decisively. The staff members can thereby minimize their sense of victimization and attendant feelings of anger toward the inmate. It is important that the employee return to a "neutral stance" as soon as possible (Gediman and Lieberman, 1996).

Of course, new employees are the most vulnerable to deception and manipulation by inmates. For example, inmates use the isolation and inexperience of new housing unit officers to con the "rookie" into permitting or failing to prevent forbidden activities and to engage in the sport of making fun of other staff members (Kauffman, 1988). The experienced employee can also fall prey to an inmate con, especially if he or she tries to initiate a manipulation. Correctional officers who attempt to "con the con" occasionally succeed in a single instance. However, once this deception becomes known, everything they do or say will be scrutinized by inmates for evidence of deceit. As a consequence, they will find their credibility shattered, their authority eroded, and their ability to persuade undermined (Kauffman, 1988). Readers are urged to never try to beat inmates at the con game. They have years of practice and hours upon hours to create and perfect their cons.

Direct Challenge and Confrontation of Manipulation

Consistent with the recommendation that staff respond promptly and decisively to inmate manipulation, it makes sense that such behavior should be confronted directly and forcefully. Right? Not necessarily. Confrontation is certainly an important strategy in the management of deception and manipulation, but it must be exercised carefully and discretely. Directly challenging an inmate's veracity can easily lead to a power struggle, from which staff seldom comes away a winner. For example, imagine the following interaction between a male inmate and a female housing unit officer:

Inmate:	Who did you vote for in the presidential election?
Officer:	You're trying to manipulate me into giving up personal information.
Inmate:	I simply asked you a question.
Officer:	Don't lie to me. You want to bring me down to your level.
Inmate:	Lady, I don't know what your problem is, but you don't need to fly off the handle.
Officer:	One more word out of you, and it's a write-up!
Inmate:	Do what you've got to do, and I'll do the same.
Officer:	Is that a threat?
Inmate:	No. It means that I'm going to file a grievance on you.
Officer:	Just be sure you spell my name right.

Notice how this brief encounter escalated into a power struggle in which the officer lost her composure and did exactly what she said she would not do: reduce herself to the inmate's level. It is questionable whether she should have responded to the inmate's question in such a confrontive manner in the first place. Assuming that he did have an ulterior motive, the officer's response resembled an attack which, by definition, invites a defensive response or counterattack.

Moreover, it is conventional wisdom that staff members should never back inmates into a corner, especially if other inmates are around. In this particular scenario, the officer might have been better off using one of the "three Rs" to be discussed later in this chapter.

So, just what is the appropriate way to directly challenge, or confront, inmate manipulation? The authors prefer to view confrontation as pointing out to inmates the inconsistencies in their statements or actions. In fact, one way to conceive of confrontation is to consider it a special form of constructive criticism containing a mixture of observation and suggestion (Fautek, 2001). For example, consider the following conversation between an inmate and his General Equivalency Degree (GED) instructor:

Inmate: I want to drop out of school. I'll never get my GED.

Instructor: You told us last week that nothing was more important to you than earning a GED.

Inmate: Nah, I couldn't have said that. I've always known I'd never get it.

Instructor: That's interesting, because just yesterday you were talking about how proud your mother was that you'd be the first person in your family to graduate from high school or earn a GED.

Inmate: Yeah, well, that was yesterday and this is today.

Instructor: So, which is it? Are you going to follow through with your goal or take the easy way out?

Observe how the instructor positively but persistently challenges the inmate to examine the inconsistencies in his various statements. (Notice, too, that the inmate's remarks reflect two criminal thinking patterns which often coexist: cognitive indolence and discontinuity.) Compare and contrast the instructor's confrontation with that of the officer in the preceding vignette.

The instructor's responses are consistent with Dutton's (1995) view of confrontation. Confrontation should provide the recipient with a different and challenging perspective on his or her behavior and never should be used as a means of attack nor an effort to tear the person down. Goldring (1997) suggests that confrontation is often most effective when it catches persons by surprise and exposes dramatic discrepancies between their attitudes and behavior. Confrontation, when used appropriately, can be a highly effective method for managing inmates' deception and manipulation. Here are some illustrations of confrontation in a prison setting:

1) **Pointing out the disparity between verbal responses.** For example, "You say that you don't give a damn about your family, but you're always the first one to ask if you received any mail."
2) **Pointing out the discrepancy between emotions and verbal responses.** For example, "You say that you accept the warden's decision to deny your furlough, but your voice is loud and your teeth are clenched."
3) **Identifying the conflict between a verbal response and that which would be expected from a noncriminal.** For example, "I noticed that you and the other inmates clapped when you heard that a police officer was killed last night. Is that the reaction most people would have?"
4) **Calling attention to obvious "game playing."** For example, "You say you want to get your life together, but I hear that you're making jokes about the (treatment) program and you're stealing things from other inmates on the unit."
5) **Questioning or challenging expectations about what is happening or might happen in the future.** For example, "Do you really believe that you can pick right back up where you left off

(with your wife) since you haven't even talked to her in six months (because she put a block on her phone)?"

No discussion of effective confrontation would be complete without examining the importance of identifying and challenging criminal thinking patterns. (Interestingly, without realizing it, the staff members in the first four examples cited above were confronting discontinuity, while the employee in the fifth illustration was challenging the inmate's superoptimistic thinking.) The confrontation of criminal thinking is especially crucial in prison treatment programs since the eight patterns shield the inmate from honest self-examination (Walters, 1990). Elliott and Walters (1991, 1997) offer suggestions for confronting these patterns in inmates participating in prison treatment programs.

Before discussing the "three Rs," we briefly comment on another way to directly challenge inmate deception and manipulation. This approach involves the disputation of irrational beliefs which interfere with the inmate's ability to follow rules, work, participate in treatment, or otherwise successfully adjust to prison life. For example, countless inmates subscribe to the notion that "life should be fair." This irrational belief inevitably results in conflict with staff and other inmates. Maultsby (1975) has formulated five criteria to determine the validity or rationality of such a belief:

1) The belief is based on observable fact.
2) The belief is likely to preserve one's health and life.
3) The belief enables one to achieve his or her immediate and long-term goals.
4) The belief allows one to avoid significant conflict with others.
5) The belief helps one feel the way he or she wants to feel.

Marek (2000) advises that if the belief fails to meet most of these criteria, it is deemed irrational and counterproductive and should be replaced with a rational one. Other irrational beliefs commonly embraced by inmates include "life should be fun (all the time)," "I deserve respect," and "life should be easy." In a prison setting such unrealistic expectations invariably lead to interpersonal conflict and should, therefore, be actively disputed. Such, disputation, like any confrontation, should be presented in a courteous, nonsarcastic, and otherwise constructive manner.

The Three Rs of Managing Deception and Manipulation

The authors frequently have successfully defended themselves against inmate manipulation through the strategic employment of the three Rs: reversal of responsibility, relabeling, and redirection. These three skills, based on Harry Vorrath and Larry Brendtro's (1974) work with juvenile offenders, enable staff to respond to inmate ploys in a powerful yet nonpunitive and nonsarcastic manner. The effective use of the three Rs will not only protect an employee from deception and exploitation, but will actually command inmate respect.

Relabeling

Conventional wisdom says that prison inmates value and even demand respect from peers, staff, their families, and everyone else. Moreover, it was established in Chapter 2 that inmates tend to see themselves as powerful figures and view other people as either strong or weak. Therefore, it makes sense that one way to foil an inmate's attempt to con a staff member is to relabel such behavior in terms which are inconsistent with the inmate's self-perception as a powerful person.

For example, suppose that an inmate approaches his counselor with a request which will require the employee to violate institutional policy. One way the counselor could respond is to say: "Why are you disrespecting me by asking me to do something that you know will get me into trouble?" This single question not only derails the inmate's manipulative effort, but essentially accuses him of doing the very thing (showing disrespect) to someone which he would not tolerate from somebody else. Typically, inmates whose behavior is relabeled in this manner will deny or minimize such disrespect, but will refrain from any further attempts to con the staff member.

What makes relabeling so effective is that it taps into values (for example, respect) which are universally embraced by the inmate population. Other ways that manipulation and deception can be relabeled include the following:

Hurtful versus Helpful
Weak versus Strong
Immature versus Mature
Cowardly versus Courageous
Selfish versus Considerate
Destructive versus Constructive
Dishonest versus Honest
Irresponsible versus Responsible
Victim versus Survivor

Few inmates, regardless of how manipulative they might wish to be, want to view or have others view their behavior as hurtful, weak, cowardly, and so forth. For example, consider the following dialog between an inmate who is trying to get a housing unit officer to tear up a disciplinary report the officer has written on the inmate's roommate:

Inmate:	"Miss Jones, I can't believe you're actually writing Connie up on such a petty issue."
Officer:	"This matter doesn't concern you, Wanda."
Inmate:	"Connie's my friend and I care about everything that happens to her."
Officer:	"Do you think that playing defense attorney for her is really being a friend?"
Inmate:	"What do you mean?"
Officer:	"To me, you're actually hurting Connie if you don't want to see Connie learn to assume responsibility for her behavior."

Inmate:	"So you're saying I'm not her friend?"
Officer:	"I'm saying that if you really cared about Connie, you'd agree that she needs to follow the rules just like you and everyone else."

Notice how the officer recasts the inmate's attempt to stand up for her friend in an unfavorable light. The offender is clearly confounded by the officer's assertion that the offender's behavior is inconsistent with her professed friendship. The offender bristles at the notion that she could actually be hurting rather than helping her friend. Therein lies the power of relabeling. The offender is forced to reexamine his or her behavior in a different light, and the staff member has preempted a power struggle with the inmate. Rather than becoming irritated by an offender's troublesome behavior (in this case playing Perry Mason for her friend), it is much more useful for staff to point out the injury one is causing to self and others (Mark and Faude, 1997).

Putting a negative spin on behavior which the inmates consider positive is only one way of relabeling. Another way of employing this powerful strategy is to reframe resistant or otherwise troublesome behavior in a positive context. For example, treatment staff are often confronted by inmates who want to blame their criminal behavior on peer pressure, poor parenting, poverty, and so forth. A therapeutic stance that views such alleged disadvantage as "opportunities" and "challenges" can often help break through such denial or resistance (McCann, 1998). After all, no one gets through life unscathed; some disadvantages, unfairness, and other distress is inherent in the human condition (Firestone, 1997).

Redirection

Inmate manipulation is frequently an attempt to distract or divert staff members from the task at hand. For example, one inmate may create a minor disturbance in a housing unit or work area to distract the officer's attention from his or her post long enough for another inmate to engage in some kind of prohibited behavior. We see such diversionary maneuvers most commonly in counseling, educational, or other treatment contexts wherein the objective is to defocus the counselor or teacher from the issue under discussion or lesson under review. If successful with this ploy, the inmate is able to avoid the hard work associated with self-examination, reading, doing arithmetic problems, and so forth.

The skill, or strategy, of redirection involves the counselor's, teacher's, or officer's ability to maintain the focus of attention on the current topic, lesson, or task (Goldring, 1997). This can be accomplished in a number of ways, of course, but must always be done quickly since the criminal thinking pattern of discontinuity enables the inmate to lose the focus on constructive activities and pursue self-serving goals without any sense of internal conflict. Moreover, once inmates fall out of sync with their stated goals, they can spin out of control very rapidly and become a nuisance to both staff and other inmates. Following are some scenarios in which the staff member effectively redirects an inmate's attention to the task at hand.

Inmate in GED Classroom: "Hey, Mr. Collins (teacher), when will we be discussing the (presidential) election? Things are really heating up down there in Florida!"

GED Instructor: "I'm glad you're interested in current events, but right now we need to review your homework from yesterday."

****

Inmate in Counseling Group: "Hey, Dr. Reynolds (psychologist), Mr. Barnaby (drug treatment counselor) has a copy of *28 Days*. Why don't you see if he'll let you borrow it so we can see it this morning?"

Psychologist: "That might be something to consider later on, but today's agenda calls for developing a relapse prevention plan."

****

Inmate in Dormitory TV Area: "Sgt. Foster, would you mind walking down to my cell and telling me if my room will pass inspection?"

Housing Unit Officer: "Van Horn (inmate), I'm getting ready to pass out mail. I'll look at your room later if I have time, but you already know the inspection standards."

In these three examples, the staff members quickly and decisively resisted efforts by the inmates to distract or divert the focus from what they (staff) were doing or planned to do. The reader can speculate about the inmate's ulterior motive in each case, but the underlying criminal thinking patterns are readily apparent. For instance, in the first scenario, the inmate tries to manipulate the teacher into using class time for what might be entertaining but otherwise irrelevant and unproductive. Such a maneuver reflects a power orientation as well as cognitive indolence in that the inmate may not only be trying to get out of work (cognitive indolence) but covertly take over control of the class (power orientation) as well.

In the second vignette, the inmate is trying to con the psychologist into letting the group watch a movie rather than tackling the challenging task of developing a plan to avoid substance abuse relapse. This is a textbook illustration of cognitive indolence. Elliott and Walters (1991) provide specific strategies for responding to inmate demands for movies, videotapes, and other sources of entertainment in group counseling. In the third example, the inmate may be plotting some mischief (cognitive indolence) or may be trying to divert the officer's attention to allow a fellow inmate to engage in prohibited conduct, possibly even assaulting another inmate (power orientation). The housing unit officer preempted either outcome by remaining focused on his primary task (passing out mail).

Two other approaches to redirection are worth noting. First, sometimes it is useful to directly point out to the inmate that he or she is focusing on the wrong priority. For example, consider the following exchange:

Inmate:	"I want to work on my English lesson today. I'm tired of doing math."
GED Instructor:	"You need to work a little longer on your math. That's the area where your pretest scores are the lowest."

The reader will notice that the teacher not only challenges the inmate's cognitive indolence, but offers encouragement and support as well. Second, a staff member can simply ignore an inmate's attempt to change the subject or divert attention from the task at hand. Such a response must be used carefully, however, since some inmates will escalate their efforts to distract staff and create a potentially disruptive situation.

Reversal of Responsibility

The reader will recall from Chapters 2 and 3 that mollification is the criminal thinking pattern whereby inmates attempt to assign responsibility for their irresponsible behavior to something or someone else (Walters, 1990). One of the most powerful ways in which staff members can confront mollification is to reverse responsibility. Vorrath and Brendtro (1974) define a reversal as the technique of placing responsibility back on the person who has the problem rather than allowing him or her to project it outward. Just as there are an infinite number of ways in which mollification can be expressed, there are an endless array of reversal strategies.

However, all reversals have one thing in common. They place inmates in such a bind that they cannot escape the responsibility for their behavior (Elliott, 1984). Consider the following example:

Sex Offender:	"I was molested by my stepfather and my uncle. I guess I was destined to do the same thing to somebody else."
Counselor:	"I understand that you experienced adversity while growing up. However, if adversity alone caused you to molest children, then everybody

135

> who experienced such adversity would become sex offenders, but we know that they don't."

Notice that the counselor's response not only stymies the inmate's attempt at mollification, but does so in a way that is empathic and supportive. The counselor acknowledges the very real pain suffered by the offender when he was a child, but holds him accountable for the way he chose to cope with the adversity as an adult. Yochelson and Samenow (1977) unapologetically and unequivocally stand firm in their refusal to accept excuses for a criminal's irresponsibility. The skillful employment of reversals can allow the counselor to successfully confront mollification without becoming embroiled in a power struggle with an inmate. Following are several types of reversals which might be appropriate in response to a typical inmate mollification statement:

Inmate (being processed for release): "You might as well keep my cell open 'cause I'm comin' right back. You people are sendin' me back to the same place where I got in trouble before."

Possible Reversal Statements:

1. "What kind of life do you want for yourself?" This single and straightforward question places responsibility for postrelease success right back in the inmate's lap. Notice how the responding staff member deftly avoids addressing the inmate's claim that it is basically staff's fault if he recidivates because he is being returned to his previous neighborhood or city of residence. Sykes and Matza (1970) refer to this type of mollification as "condemning the condemners." If the staff member had directly challenged the inmate's projection of blame, an endless and unproductive debate would have ensued. Instead, the inmate was essentially asked if he had the courage to do what he needed to do regardless of where he lives upon his release.
2. "Will such an attitude (that you are doomed to fail) help you or hurt you?" This question forces the inmate to carefully

examine the way in which he is setting himself up for failure. As in the previous response, this reversal does not even acknowledge the inmate's complaint. Instead, the inmate is encouraged to evaluate the rationality of his situation. In this way, he is directed to assume ownership of his thoughts and his behavior. Teaching inmates that they are responsible for what they think, as well as what they do, is of critical importance since antisocial behavior is largely a product of criminal thinking patterns (Walters,1990, 1994; Yochelson and Samenow, 1976).

3. "Only time will tell what choice you will make." Again, the staff member ignores the inmate's reference to staff responsibility and instead takes the position that it is the inmate's life, and what he chooses to do with it will be borne out over time (Sharp, 2000). The message to the inmate is that it is up to him to find a responsible way of meeting his needs and achieving his stated goals. Samenow (1984) encourages correctional workers to use the phrase "time will tell" to remind the inmate that assuming responsibility for his or her behavior is a continuous process.

These are but a few of the possible responses by which a staff member could reverse responsibility to the inmate for his own behavior. In addition, the three responses can be phrased in numerous ways with equal potency. All of them, however, are intended to convey to inmates the message that they alone are responsible for their own choices and behavior. Some employees will become more adept than others at the creative use of reversals.

However, under no circumstances should a reversal contain or imply any ridicule, anger, or sarcasm (Sharp, 2000). Moreover, reversals are not to be confused with the popular notion of "reverse psychology," which is occasionally humorous but often condescending. Likewise, the effective use of this strategy requires much more than simply answering a question with another question.

Additional Management Strategies

So far, the authors have presented an in-depth examination of two primary methods by which correctional staff can effectively manage inmate deception and manipulation: direct confrontation and employment of the three Rs. The remainder of this chapter is devoted to a brief review of a number of other management strategies. The first collection of strategies consists of those with which staff can prevent successful inmate manipulation, whereas the second set offers damage control suggestions to staff who discover that they have already been conned or deceived. Staff are urged to remember that, despite their best efforts to protect themselves against deception and manipulation, they can and will be conned by inmates from time to time.

Prevention Strategies

Trust Your Intuition. Prison staff frequently have the sense that something about an interaction with an inmate just does not feel right. Rarely, however, does an employee stop to examine the basis of such a "gut feeling." Gavin De Becker (1997, 1999), however, contends that one's intuitive reactions to situations are usually accurate and that "gut feelings" are actually based on observations and perceptions that are not processed at a level of cognitive awareness.

Allen and Bonta (1981) observe that staff members' feelings represent an aspect of corrections that should never be ignored or set aside without careful analysis. They should pay especially close attention to their intuition if it is experienced as an "uh-oh" feeling. Such a reaction may well indicate that they are being manipulated (Simon, 1996).

Pay Close Attention to Inmate's Normal Behavior. The importance of nonverbal behavior is such that no discussion of deceit and manipulation can be intelligently pursued without considering this channel of communication (Ford, 1996). However, the reader must be warned that there is no one sign of deceit—no facial expression or muscle twitch that in and of itself means that an inmate (or anybody else) is lying. To make matters worse, individuals with antisocial personalities, including many if not most prison inmates, are the very people whose normal behavior may be most difficult to decipher. Since their lies are not associated with guilt, there are fewer nonverbal signs to betray their deceit (Ford, 1996). Moreover, inmates will sometimes wear dark glasses to hide as much of their face as possible thus obscuring their deception. Nevertheless, the astute staff member may be able to perceive some evidence of conning or lying by closely attending to an inmate's speech patterns, facial expressions, and body movements.

Be Aware of Your Own Nonverbal Behavior. It is conventional wisdom within corrections that inmates carefully monitor staff members' movements and facial expressions. The inmate who is seeking to manipulate an employee continuously "reads" the latter's nonverbal behavior and, in response to such "feedback," adjusts his or her own behavior to make the deception more credible (Ford, 1996). For example, if an inmate asks an employee for a favor and the employee responds to the request by stuttering, breaking eye contact, and/or stepping away, the staff member's actual verbal reply is largely unimportant. The inmate will infer from the employee's nonverbal behavior that a successful manipulation is likely. Allen and Bonta (1981) observe that inmates are consistently on the lookout for staff members who cannot come across with any degree of firmness in their interaction with inmates. Such employees are regarded as easily conned. (Incidently, the authors have noted that staff who tend to overlook minor rule infractions by inmates are at an even higher risk for manipulation.) Accordingly, correctional employees are encouraged to remain keenly aware of their nonverbal behavior at all times when communicating with inmates. How they come across is more important than what they say.

Be Honest and Direct When Talking with Inmates. Having just established the critical nature of nonverbal behavior, the authors now turn their attention to the verbal content of staff member communications with inmates. Employees must understand that they actually set the stage for manipulation by the manner in which they talk with inmates. For example, some employees subscribe to the misguided notion that the best way to communicate with inmates is to use profanity and convict jargon, or participate in mutual joking or story telling. Nothing could be further from the truth. Not only do inmates lose respect for staff who engage in such behavior, but they view them as easy prey for deception and manipulation.

The authors frequently have found that cordial, direct, and limited verbal interaction enhances one's credibility which limits the likelihood of exploitation by inmates. Staff members who talk in circles, say too much, or come across as "wishy washy" when talking with inmates, are vulnerable to manipulation. For instance, it is not uncommon for an inmate in a treatment program to ask the counselor to write a letter of recommendation to the parole board and exaggerate the inmate's accomplishments in treatment. Pollock (1998) believes that the counselor should inform the inmate in no uncertain terms that he or she will not "sugarcoat" or misrepresent the facts in a letter. Elliott and Walters (1991) go as far as to recommend against even writing such a letter in the first place, since completion of any treatment program does not guarantee future prosocial behavior.

We suggest that staff responses to all inmate requests be simple, clear, and structured. Inmates will generally respond favorably to communication delivered in this manner and will have no opening through which to attempt manipulation. Indeed, the authors remain impressed by the degree to which inmates can be persuaded to follow rules and otherwise cooperate when staff "shoot straight" with them, especially when denying requests or giving orders. Kauffman (1988) has noted that correctional officers are able to dissuade inmates from engaging in prohibited conduct through the use of fair, consistent, and rational communication.

Seek Collateral Information. Whenever possible, staff members are encouraged to find out as much as they can about the inmates in their housing unit, classroom, counseling groups, work area, or elsewhere. Many inmates are masters of deception and can present themselves in a favorable light, especially when they want something (Samenow, 1984). Therefore, correctional employees need to rely on something other than the inmate's self-report before granting a request or a favor. Reading the inmate's central file, directly observing his or her behavior in different situations, or talking with other staff who know the inmate are all methods in which the staff member can make an informed decision regarding the request. For example, taking the time to read the inmate's presentence investigation report not only can provide valuable insight into an inmate's background and criminal history, but it also can offer objective facts against which self-reports can be verified or refuted (White, 1999). Likewise, talking with other staff about inmates can generate information which can be used as a benchmark against which to judge the inmate's veracity.

The authors have found that inmates' requests for special accommodations, such as housing unit changes or job reassignments should be closely examined for the existence of an ulterior motive. For example, the first author was recently approached by an inmate who requested his assistance in transferring to another housing unit. The inmate met the criteria for placement in the requested unit, but the author solicited the input of the inmate's unit manager who advised that the inmate had "broken up" with his homosexual lover. It was determined that the requested reassignment would be inappropriate since the inmate would either try to establish a homosexual relationship with an inmate in the new housing unit, or request a transfer back to the original unit if he reconciled with his former lover. As Allen and Bonta (1981) wisely observe, when it comes to protecting oneself from deception and manipulation, "knowledge is power." Acquiring knowledge about inmates requires that staff seek information from someone other than the inmate (Salekin, 2000).

Damage Control Strategies

Stall for Time. When a staff member discovers that he or she is on the receiving end of inmate deception, there is absolutely nothing wrong with saying or doing nothing right away. Indeed, Allen and Bonta (1981) advise that it may be best for the employee to remain uncommitted rather than say or do something which might serve to

141

make the situation worse. For example, imagine a scenario in which a physician's assistant realizes that he had been conned by an inmate into authorizing an unnecessary medical idle for the day. The inmate's work supervisor, housing unit officer, and others have already been notified. The physician's assistant could certainly try to rescind the authorization and/or call the inmate to the infirmary and "read him the riot act." However, to do either could create a logistical and accountability problem for several staff, and rob the physician's assistant of valuable time better spent with other patients. By "stalling for time," the physician's assistant can reflect on the situation and decide how he could avoid being conned in a similar situation in the future, and make an entry in the inmate's medical chart cautioning other health care professionals to be wary of the inmate's manipulative tendencies.

Lick Your Wounds and Move On. This is a variation of the previous strategy, which is especially appropriate when the employee is angry or ashamed over having been duped by an inmate. It is normal and natural to feel hurt and betrayed, as well as ashamed and embarrassed, on the discovery that one has been successfully deceived or manipulated. Sometimes staff members will become so enraged that they contemplate ways to retaliate against the inmate. For example, a correctional officer in a housing unit was recently manipulated into opening a food slot through which an inmate promptly dumped his food tray. The officer became so angry that he obtained another food tray and dumped it inside the inmate's cell. Such a vindictive response is usually self-defeating since the employee has just exposed his or her "hot spots," thereby setting the stage for further exploitation. Therefore, staff who fall prey to a successful con are encouraged to walk away, reflect on the experience, and consider alternative ways to prevent future occurrences of the same or similar manipulations (Sigafoos, 1994).

Make Another Staff Member Aware. Allen and Bonta (1981) observe that when inmates attempt to deceive or manipulate staff, it is almost always when the employee is alone. This is especially true if the inmate is trying to con the staff into doing something that violates policy. The employee, immediately upon discovering that he or she has been manipulated, is advised to notify another staff member. Such notification is critical for two reasons: First, if the employee has been manipulated into doing something which violates policy, prompt notification may enable the staff member to avert or at least limit the severity of disciplinary action. Second, the inmate can be charged with committing a prohibited act and held accountable, thus possibly preventing the exploitation of other employees.

What if the manipulation does not necessarily entail the violation of institution policy? For example, imagine that an inmate has conned the segregation lieutenant into releasing him to the general population three days too soon. The lieutenant could notify the inmate's unit team or disciplinary hearing officer regarding the premature release. This could be noted in the inmate's disciplinary record, thereby decreasing the likelihood that a similar oversight could happen again. Moreover, the inmate develops or enhances his reputation as a "manipulator," which might protect other employees from deception. Regardless of the nature of the manipulation, staff members who have been conned need to discuss the situation with other employees and make sure that the inmates know that such a discussion has taken place.

Document What Happened. This guideline follows directly from the previous one. For several reasons, it is in the staff member's best interest to write a memorandum or otherwise document any instance in which he or she has been successfully manipulated by an inmate. First, if the manipulation involved a rule violation, documentation is required for any disciplinary action to be imposed. Second, a prompt and thorough accounting of the violation may protect the employee from any charges of professional misconduct and/or adverse action. Third, even if the manipulation did not violate any prohibited act, it is still important to fully document the interchange so that the inmate can be less likely to successfully con another staff member. After all, the inmate has already exhibited a propensity to play games; documentation can make it easier for another staff member to be "on guard" when interacting with the manipulator (Correia, 2000).

Maintain and Exercise a Sense of Humor. So-called "gallows" humor is prevalent among correctional personnel (Kauffman, 1988). Indeed, through exaggeration and irreverence, it is possible to distance oneself from shocking, disgusting, or dangerous situations and prevent unwanted emotional responses (Benner, 2000). Likewise, one of the most effective ways to cope with inmate deception and manipulation is to adopt a healthy sense of humor. In other words, it is useful to be able to reflect on the situation, laugh at oneself, and move on. This is especially true if the manipulation causes no substantive harm, as in the following example:

Inmate: "Ms. Adams (drug treatment specialist), the wall clock (fifteen minutes fast) says it's 3:00. Some of us have to get to early chow."

Ms. Adams: (looks at her watch) "That's odd, I've only got 2:45. I must be slow. Okay, I guess we'll stop for now. See you guys tomorrow."

Inmate: (on his way out of the classroom) "Oh, by the way, Ms. Adams, Mr. Myers (another drug treatment specialist) set the clock ahead by fifteen minutes yesterday because he didn't want to run over like he usually does."

Ms. Adams: (grinning) "Very clever, William (inmate). You got me. I'll be ready next time."

The authors cannot overstate the importance of developing a good sense of humor in dealing with prison inmates. In the preceding scenario, the drug treatment specialist called the inmate on his game-playing, but did so in a way which was free of tension, conflict, and retaliation. Moreover, she demonstrated to the inmate, and others who were probably watching, that she does not take herself too seriously and can handle being the "butt" of a joke.

Being conned or duped by an inmate can evoke feelings of humiliation and retaliatory anger in even the most seasoned correctional worker. It is useful to realize that inmates, many of whom were cons long before coming to prison, have plenty of time on their hands to plan and play games with staff. If the employee takes such deception and manipulation personally, the inmate will delight in this trickery even more and the staff member suffers a significant blow to his or her self-confidence and sense of effectiveness. Therefore, it is often useful to admit that "you got me that time," thereby conceding "defeat" and avoiding a contentious and unproductive power struggle (Ruegg, Haynes, Frances, 1997). (Avoiding power struggles is one of the "Ten Commandments" to be discussed in the next chapter.)

Chapter 9

Ten Commandments
for Prison Staff

This book has described a great many, although by no means all, examples of deception and manipulation perpetrated by prison inmates on well-meaning and unsuspecting staff. In addition, the reader was introduced in Chapter 8 to some of the ways in which he or she can avoid or at least minimize the harm caused by inmate deception and manipulation. The authors would be remiss, however, if they failed to emphasize that all prison employees—regardless of training or experience—will be conned by inmates. Indeed, readers who have worked or currently work in a prison setting have already been successfully manipulated by one or more inmates. Hopefully, the manipulation resulted in nothing more than a little embarrassment and a few laughs at oneself.

For some staff, unfortunately, the cumulative effects of being conned and duped by inmates include bitterness, disillusionment, and cynicism. Such employees are at risk for career burnout and health problems. They often create an unpleasant working atmosphere for fellow employees. The purpose of this chapter is to offer ten strategies whereby staff can remain satisfied and avoid burnout while working in an environment that is inherently adversarial and often confrontational. These strategies, based on some fifty years of correctional experience shared by the authors, are dubbed "The Ten Commandments for Prison Staff" because they are considered vital in helping an employee maintain his or her sanity, sense of dignity, and personal safety.

Commandment #1: Go Home Safe and Sound at the End of the Day.

Personal safety must take precedence over any other consideration in day-to-day contact with inmates. Unfortunately, the authors have found that all too often, staff members take unnecessary risks or become complacent in their interaction with inmates. New employees are often eager to prove to themselves and others that they are not afraid of inmates, and occasionally they become overzealous in their enforcement of rules and regulations. Seasoned employees, on the other hand, are likely to fall prey to the comfort and predictability of their work routine and let down their guard in the presence of inmates. Although the prison environment is generally more dangerous for correctional officers than treatment staff, the latter often forget where they are and place themselves in vulnerable situations (Marks, 2000). Here are some precautionary maneuvers that the authors and others have found useful in enhancing their physical safety in the correctional environment.

Know Where Help Is and How to Call for Assistance. When one is in an inmate housing unit or other areas of the prison, it is important to know the physical layout and location of the nearest exits, and where the nearest staff members and telephone can be found (Pollock, 1998).

Use Your Own "Gut Feelings" as an Assessment Tool. Does the inmate's behavior create feelings of a threat or intimidation? Is there a sense that something is "not quite right" about a request he or she is making? If so, Ruegg et al. (1997) suggests that such internal reactions shall be taken seriously, especially when dealing with someone with an antisocial personality disorder. Moreover, people typically register feelings of fear or threat when they have perceived, often unconsciously, something in the other person's behavior to justify such a reaction (De Becker, 1997, 1999). For example, a staff member may be responding to something in the inmate's voice or facial expression, which is cause for concern. The bottom line is that "gut feelings" should not be ignored or rationalized. Although it may be hard to pinpoint the basis for such feelings, intuition should be regarded as a "yellow light" when dealing with an inmate.

Don't Wait: Take Immediate Action to Insure Your Own Safety. Just as one should not ignore his or her feelings, an employee should be prepared to act on those feelings quickly and decisively. Correctional personnel sometimes believe that they must prove their mettle by handling dangerous situations by themselves. Nothing is further from the truth! One should not hesitate to exit a potentially dangerous situation and/or ask for help from other staff. To the extent possible, employees should not allow themselves to be obscured from the view of other staff (Allen and Bosta, 1981).

150

Be Alert for Warning Signs of Possible Danger. Staff should conduct periodic and thorough "spot checks" of areas under their supervision and pay attention to groupings of inmates, listening carefully for references to violence or disturbances. For example, if one overhears a casual reference to a missing knife or fire in a housing unit, he or she should investigate further and report the information to appropriate supervisory personnel (Cox, 1998).

Arrange Your Office/Work Area in a Manner Which Maximizes Your Safety. Keep objects which could be used as weapons out of sight or at least make them inaccessible to others. The first author once made the mistake of placing a bronze silhouette of a horse on his desk. It served as a reference point for establishing rapport with several inmates. Unfortunately, a mentally ill person picked it up and brandished it as a weapon. (The author now relies on other means of building rapport!) It is also important that furniture be positioned so that it does not impede your exit from the office/area in the event that an inmate becomes violent. Moreover, a staff member should not remain in a room alone with an agitated inmate; the employee should call for assistance and wait for help to arrive.

Dress with Your Personal Safety in Mind. Correctional workers need to consider the degree to which their clothing compromises their personal safety. For example, female staff should wear clothes that are neither too tight nor revealing, while male staff should consider wearing breakaway, clip-on ties (Simon, 1996). Also, correctional employees should carry functional radios or body alarms at all times.

Share Your Experiences with Other Staff. At one time or another, nearly all correctional employees will have a harrowing experience involving a threat to their personal safety. Something can be learned from each of these experiences, so it is useful to openly discuss such situations and examine how they were handled and might have been prevented (Walker, 1994). For example, several years ago, a female penitentiary psychologist found herself with an agitated inmate following a 12-step meeting. The outer door to the psychology department had already been secured by the corridor officer who had erroneously assumed that all inmates had exited the area. The inmate began to assault the psychologist who had left her body alarm on her desk. She managed to maneuver herself to the desk and attempted to activate the alarm; unfortunately, it malfunctioned. The inmate, in a textbook display of superoptimism, grabbed the alarm, pressed the activation button repeatedly, and taunted the psychologist with sarcastic remarks about shoddy equipment and the ineptitude of staff. The inmate was unaware, however, that he had inadvertently activated the alarm. Within seconds, the "cavalry" came to the rescue and the psychologist averted serious injury. She now regularly shares this experience and the lessons learned from it with new employees.

Commandment #2:
Establish Realistic Expectations.

As many as 50 to 75 percent of prison inmates meet the diagnostic criteria for antisocial personality disorder (Hare, 1996). That means that they are restless, impulsive, contemptuous, untrustworthy, unreliable, and oppositional. It is certainly understandable, therefore, why staff who work with such individuals become easily frustrated and discouraged. To new employees especially, the irresponsibility, lack of cooperation, and limited insight displayed by offenders can come as a disheartening surprise (Black, 1999).

Unfortunately, the antisocial values and criminal identity embraced by many offenders are "carved in stone" (Hare, 1993). There is little likelihood that anything staff can do will produce fundamental, long-term changes. Even when inmates promise to change and make short-term improvement in their behavior, staff will become bitterly disappointed if they allow themselves to believe that permanent changes have occurred (Hare, 1993). Accordingly, it is imperative that correctional employees learn to expect inmates to be uncooperative and resistant. Otherwise, they will find themselves doing "hard time" right along with the inmate.

Counselors and other treatment staff are especially vulnerable to disillusionment and despair in their work with inmates. Many young, well-educated men and women enter corrections with enthusiasm and commitment, only to grow disenchanted and experience a sense of futility because their efforts do not achieve desired results (Yochelson and Samenow, 1976). Sadly, some decide that they no longer want any part of working with criminals. Unfortunately, their expectations were based on the faulty assumption that offenders adhere to the same values that prosocial individuals embrace (Sharp, 2000). That is simply not the case. Many offenders fear intimacy, cannot accept criticism, and resent anyone who attempts to challenge their behavior (Simon, 1996). It is simply unrealistic to expect that such a person will be capable of acknowledging the need for change on the basis of internalized values for a long time, if ever (Ruegg et al., 1997).

How then, are correctional counselors, psychologists, drug abuse treatment specialists, and other mental health professionals supposed to maintain interest in and commitment to their work and avoid the disillusionment discussed in the previous paragraph? The authors recommend that treatment staff find a way to redefine "success" in their work with offenders. Recidivism, while obviously important, is only one way of assessing the effectiveness of treatment efforts. Here are three other ways in which treatment staff can redefine outcome goals and thus establish realistic expectations for both themselves and inmates:

1. Acknowledge that it is all right for an inmate to enter into treatment for reasons other than the desire to change. For example, an offender may seek to "look good" for a parole board or earn an early release from confinement through the completion of treatment programs. His or her only desire may be to perform adequately enough to obtain a certificate of completion or a favorable recommendation. Treatment staff should regard such external motivation as a legitimate reason to enter treatment (Walters, 1990) and hope that the inmate may, over time, internalize the values and concepts being transmitted through the program. However, even if he or she does not, program

participation may at least help keep the offender busy and out of trouble in prison. Indeed, Innes (1997) has found that inmate participation in residential treatment programs results in a significant reduction in disciplinary reports.

2. A good argument can be made that treatment is successful if it moves an individual to a higher level of either cognitive or emotional functioning (Pollock, 1998). For example, what about an offender who, after completing a prison treatment program, reoffends, but does so in a less socially harmful way? Perhaps the offender is arrested for simple drug possession rather than his or her original crime: armed robbery. This can and should be regarded as evidence of at least modest treatment effectiveness.

3. Given the stubbornness and denial of most offenders, treatment staff should take pride in and solace from the fact that a small number of inmates who complete programs do not, in fact, reoffend. This is especially important to remember in sex offender treatment, when even "one victim less is a success" (Lea, Auburn, and Kibblewhite, 1999).

The bottom line suggested for clinicians who work with inmates is to anticipate the obstacles and complexities inherent in treating these difficult inmates and adjust expectations accordingly. Indeed, Stone (2000) maintains that one of the ideal qualities for working with antisocial individuals is the ability to avoid excessive expectations for their improvement. After all, there is a big difference between being a good therapist and being a "miracle worker" (Fautek, 2001).

Commandment #3:
Set Firm and Consistent Limits.

Regardless of the position held by a correctional employee, he or she can expect inmates to engage in limit-testing. The testing of limits is a slow and often subtle process of "pushing, bending, breaking, and circumventing minor rules to determine how far the manipulation can go before an employee takes action" (Allen and Bosta, 1981, p. 50). The goal is to determine how quickly, how easily, and how much the staff member will give. So how does an employee effectively respond to limit-testing behavior? Sharp (2000, p. 83) offers the following guidelines for staff:

> (Our) relationship with criminals is built on expectations, accountability, and responsibility. They (inmates) can expect us to do what we say we will do. We are consistent in the application (of) and response to violation of rules. We treat them with respect and dignity. We are firm, fair, and friendly—not friends— friendly. And we expect them to be and do the same. We are clear about our expectations and consequences.
>
> Through adherence to these guidelines, an employee will earn and command the respect of inmates throughout the institution. Moreover, the staff member is less likely to be conned or duped by an inmate into doing something illegal or unethical. The employee will earn a reputation as someone with integrity and credibility who is dedicated to maintaining the safety of both staff and inmates and the security and orderly running of the prison.

Even though the importance of limit-setting is obvious for correctional officers and work supervisors, it is just as important for treatment staff. For example, inmates in residential drug treatment programs are notorious for trying to take over the leadership of counseling groups, find ways to avoid fulfilling assigned responsibilities, and otherwise usurp staff authority and circumvent program expectations (Elliott and Walters, 1997). Yochelson and Samenow (1977) observe that the counselor has no hope of being successful if he or she allows the inmate to set the conditions for treatment. They, like Elliott and Walters (1997), note that inmates will try to manage others, whether in individual or group counseling, and try to maneuver the program to suit themselves. Therefore, the counselor must stand firm and not allow the inmate to do this; otherwise, he or she will be seen as weak and indecisive (Yochelson and Samenow, 1977).

Moreover, by insisting that inmates comply with the requirements and time commitment of their treatment, the chances of a successful therapy outcome are enhanced (Hadley, Reddon, and Reddick). Attendance, punctuality, active participation in group discussion, and completion of homework assignments are all aspects of treatment compliance for which inmates should be held accountable.

Setting limits on disruptive or off-task behavior should be another priority for treatment staff. This can be quite difficult at times and requires intestinal fortitude and finesse. Employment of the three Rs—reversal of responsibility, relabeling, and redirection—can be extremely useful in this context. In group counseling, the group itself can be a powerful tool for limit-setting, although the counselor or therapist must watch out for group members who are excessively tyrannical (Rose, 1998). Of course, inmates with psychopathic tendencies or antisocial personalities will sometimes try to manipulate the counselor and drive him or her out of the treatment role. With these inmates, who are often charming and engaging, therapists are tempted to make exceptions to established rules of treatment (Simon, 1996). If the counselor takes the bait, he or she has committed a major error in the management of interpersonal boundaries with inmates (an issue to be discussed in detail later in this chapter). Oldham and Russakoff (1989) advocate the use of especially clear and firm limit setting for this type of inmate.

Commandment #4:
Avoid Power Struggles.

As noted in Chapter 2, power is one of the five basic needs which motivate human behavior (Glasser, 2000). Moreover, the power orientation (Walters, 1990) is one of the eight criminal thinking patterns with which staff will be confronted on a daily basis in their work with inmates. For example, Chapter 4 was devoted to various ways in which inmates attempt to assert power and achieve control at the expense of staff. It is crucial that correctional employees understand that engaging in power struggles with an inmate, especially a psychopathic one, is risky business. This is because inmates are experts at setting up conflict situations in which they will emerge as the winner (Hare, 1993).

At this point, the reader may be wondering how the inmate can realistically expect to "win" a struggle for power control with staff. After all, staff have the keys, the weapons, and everything else they need to be in charge, right? In the long run, this is true. However, it must be remembered that, as Yochelson and Samenow (1977) observe, criminals are sprinters, not long distance runners. Therefore, their efforts to gain power and control must be understood within the context of a very limited time horizon. For example, why would an inmate refuse to come out of his or her cell when there is no doubt whatsoever that prison staff will eventually "win?"

Why do inmates destroy their own cells and housing units when they are the ones who suffer afterward? In both instances, the inmates are inconveniencing staff, generating considerable excitement for both themselves and other inmates, and directing attention to their "cause." In other words, they have achieved a sense of power and gained some semblance of control, if only for a short period of time (Pollock, 1998).

In addition to settling for limited "victories" in their day-to-day coexistence with staff, it is useful to remember that the inmate's whole life has been based on power and control—gaining or losing it (Sharp, 2000). Therefore, correctional employees should be careful that they do not respond to the inevitable power plays by inmates in a manner which makes the situation worse.

For example, staff can be direct and firm without being provocative and forcing the inmate into a corner out of which attack is the only perceived option. It is also important that staff avoid using manipulative tactics in their own efforts to assert or regain power over inmates. First of all, most employees are not nearly as sophisticated at the art of manipulation; in other words, it is unlikely that they can successfully "con the con." Moreover, even if a manipulative ploy is successful in a single instance, once it is discovered it usually leads to a decrease in the staff member's power and credibility. This is because inmates will thereafter scrutinize the employee's words and actions for signs of deceit, thereby undermining the latter's ability to persuade and eroding his or her authority (Kauffman, 1988).

Psychologists, counselors, and other mental health professionals must be aware of the need to avoid power struggles with inmates during the treatment process. One important power struggle to avoid is trying to convince the inmate that he or she needs treatment or to attempt to "sell" the offender on the idea that therapy would be "good" for him or her (Decker, 1999). Instead, counselors should focus on creating the conditions under which inmates decide for themselves that treatment is in their best interest. Flores (1997) cautions that confrontations by the therapist only work when they are motivational and facilitative in nature. It is also wise for treatment staff to avoid being embroiled in useless and counterproductive debates over intellectual or philosophical ideas.

Some inmates are quarrelsome during counseling sessions to "bait" counselors into circular arguments or to prove a point of little or no significance. Fault finding and dogmatic, such inmates achieve special delight in contradicting or embarrassing the counselor or therapist (Millon and Davis, 1998). By the same token, treatment staff are ill-advised to engage in unnecessary bickering over the "facts" surrounding an incident or the truthfulness of an inmate's account of his or her past (Mark and Faude, 1997). Nobody will accomplish anything in treatment if the inmates feel as if they have to fight staff. If a counselor gets into a particularly heated power struggle with an inmate, he or she should apologize and indicate that it was unintended (Sharp, 2000).

Commandment #5:
Manage Interpersonal Boundaries.

A hallmark of the psychologically healthy person is the ability to establish and maintain good personal boundaries. This essentially involves knowing where one stops and another person begins (Simon, 1996). Nowhere is boundary management more important than is working with prison inmates. Correctional employees must directly confront any comment made, question posed, or action displayed by an inmate which has the potential to weaken the boundary which separates staff and inmates. Staff members must consistently monitor their response to seemingly casual remarks from inmates who, as emphasized throughout this book, have a self-serving, ulterior motive for almost everything they do or say. There are at least three ways in which staff can unwittingly permit boundaries to be violated by inmates: 1) confusing friendliness with familiarity; 2) disclosing personal information; and 3) participating in conversations of a sexual nature.

1. **Friendliness versus Familiarity:** Correctional employees, like any professionals, are expected to be friendly and courteous. However, inmates often interpret excessive friendliness as a weakness to be exploited. Therefore, staff must make a distinction in their mind and outward behavior between friendliness and familiarity (Allen and Bosta, 1981). An obvious example of familiarity is discussing any kind of personal or financial problem with or in the vicinity of inmates. One of the most frequent forms of familiarity, but one that is often unrecognized as such, is permitting inmates to address staff by their first names. Almost without exception, an inmate who believes that he or she can call an employee by his or her first name sooner or later will attempt to curry favor from the staff member. This is an especially important issue for treatment staff, for whom boundaries with inmates can become easily blurred. Simon (1996) observes that treatment effectiveness is unlikely when the client addresses the therapist on a first-name basis because the former does not accept his or her role as that of a client. Another example of excessive familiarity is the "chatty relationship" (Mark and Faude, 1997) in which an employee and inmate have a relationship which promotes an atmosphere of barroom banter. Such a relationship is conducive to gossip, rumors, and the leakage of sensitive information.

2. **Self-Disclosure:** Inmates have an uncanny ability to discover a staff member's weaknesses and vulnerabilities to "pitch the con" to them (Ford, 1996). Unfortunately, some employees make the inmate's job easier by revealing their vulnerabilities through excessive self-disclosure. For example, a psychologist who was supervising an Alcoholics Anonymous meeting disclosed that she had "partied" quite a bit while attending college. One of the inmates who attended the meeting spread a rumor that the psychologist was a recovering alcoholic and, therefore, had no business counseling inmates on their substance abuse problems. Many inmates thrive on taking such revelations by staff out of context and using them for self-serving or malicious purposes.

Indeed, psychopathic inmates are especially likely to "build dossiers" on staff for exploitative purposes at a later date (Kernberg, 1998). Therefore, correctional employees are advised to be very careful with what they disclose to inmates or to other staff in the presence of inmates (Sharp, 2000).Correctional staff are trained and expected to be fair, direct, and honest with inmates. Honesty, however, does not mean the same thing as self-disclosure (Meloy, 1988).

Employees must constantly ask themselves if and when it is appropriate to disclose personal information they should disclose to inmates. The staff member must be certain that he or she is not revealing something that can be misused. This is a tall order, because even seemingly innocuous self-disclosures can backfire.

For example, a novice drug treatment specialist shared with inmates in a counseling group that she was trying, albeit unsuccessfully, to quit smoking. Within minutes, group members were asking her if her boyfriend found kissing her to be unpleasant. She recognized this as a significant boundary violation, but was at a loss regarding how to respond. (She had not yet been trained in the use of the three Rs.) Cullari (1996) recommends that self-disclosure be used only if the staff member has a strategic purpose in mind. Finally, and for reasons which will become clear in the next section, correctional staff should not disclose sexual thoughts, fantasies, or experiences with inmates.

3. **Sexual Reference:** Research has demonstrated that even casual discussions of sex with members of the opposite gender is often a prelude to sexual misconduct in the workplace (Simon, 1996). Such a progression from talk to action evolves over a lengthy period of time, during which interpersonal boundaries are systematically eroded. Typically, the process works like this: An inmate approaches a staff member and makes an allusion to sex simply to determine the employee's reaction. Initially, the inmate is careful not to direct the sexual reference toward the staff member (Allen and Bosta, 1981). If the employee appears aroused or otherwise receptive to such comments, the inmate will feel empowered to continue the dialog and become increasingly intimate. Some nonsexual touching may ensue and, before long, the employee spends long periods of time, often in private, talking with the inmate about personal matters.

For example, an inmate approached a female psychologist after a therapy group session and told her that one of the other inmates in the group was sexually fantasizing about her. The psychologist profusely thanked the inmate for the information and asked him what he thought she should do about the situation. The inmate counseled the psychologist to do nothing and offered to "keep an eye" on the inmate and make sure that he did not harm her. The inmate induced the psychologist to arrange for his assignment as the janitor for the psychology department and he began to spend every day sitting outside her office while she met with other inmates. Between sessions, the psychologist allowed the inmate to sit in her office and the two would talk about mutually sensitive personal issues. The inmate, who claimed to benefit significantly from the "intensive therapy" he was receiving, started to ask for "therapeutic hugs." Other staff became suspicious when the inmate began escorting the psychologist to the sallyport area through which employees exit the institution at the end of the day. She was shocked to learn that a routine search of the inmate's cell had uncovered pages and pages of violent, sadistic, and sexually deviant fantasy material authored in his handwriting!

Although the preceding example certainly reflects poor judgment and boundary management on the part of the employee, it offers two critical insights for staff who wish to avoid such predicaments. First, physical contact with offenders is, almost without exception, a bad idea! This may be a bitter pill for some treatment staff to swallow; after all, physical touching in many counseling situations can be a powerful form of support and encouragement. Unfortunately, most inmates tend to overinterpret touching, especially from opposite-sex staff, and attach romantic or sexual significance to such contact. Indeed, even the accidental touching of an inmate's hand can be construed (by the inmate) as a "come-on" or encouragement for more aggressive sexual behavior (Albrecht, 1997).

Second, boundary violations that lead to actual or potential sexual encounters commence in a relatively benign fashion, perhaps with a compliment or flicking a dirt speck from a female employee's blouse, or straightening a male officer's shirt collar. If the employee registers no concerns, the compliments become more personal and the touching more intimate. The inmate continuously observes the staff member for signs of approval or disapproval (Allen and Bosta, 1981). Therefore, it is important that employees move quickly to deter boundary intrusions as quickly and forcefully as possible. The message should be something like this: "I do not welcome or approve of what you are doing or saying, and I expect it to stop immediately!"

The authors have devoted considerable attention to the fifth "commandment" because failure to manage boundaries with inmates can result in the end of a career, marriage, or both. It is the responsibility of all correctional staff to establish and maintain boundaries that define and secure their professional relationship with inmates. Interpersonal boundaries are not violated suddenly. Rather, the violations are gradual and progressive (Simon, 1996). Sometimes the erosion of a boundary is barely noticeable. For that reason the employee must continuously monitor his or her feelings and behavior toward inmates. If a staff member has unmet social or emotional needs, and is unsure of these processes at work, inappropriate relationships with an inmate may occur (Pollock, 1998). Unfortunately, some employees chose to engage in denial, the psychological defense mechanism that blinds one to such an extent that he or she does not even recognize that a problem exists until it has become so severe that its consequences cannot be escaped.

Commandment #6:
Do Not Take Things Personally.

In Chapter 2, the authors described a style of thinking exhibited by most inmates which underlies their antisocial behavior both outside and within prison walls. Specifically, inmates tend to see other people as pawns or chess pieces to be used to whatever advantage they feel entitled (Samenow, 1984). Inmates routinely disregard the feelings of staff members and devalue them as persons. Most inmates view noncriminals as "suckers" or "squares." Staff must remember that such a worldview is directed toward everyone—not just them. Inmates interact with and respond to everyone in the same way (Sharp, 2000). Therefore, inmate behavior—whether conning, manipulation resistance, or lying—should not be taken personally.

The reader is encouraged to understand and accept the fact that everyone, including the so-called experts, can be taken in, manipulated, conned, and bewildered by a seasoned inmate. Hare (1993) observes that a "good psychopath" can play a concerto on anyone's heartstrings.

Although not all inmates are psychopaths, most exhibit psychopathic behavior such as lying and deceit. The important point here is that such behavior is part and parcel of the inmate's lifestyle (Ford, 1996) and not a reflection of either a character deficit or professional incompetence on the part of the staff member. Indeed, despite a combined fifty years of correctional experience, the authors continue to fall prey to the games inmates play. The challenge is one of not personalizing such manipulation, but instead learning from the experience and moving on.

Correctional treatment staff are especially prone to personalizing inmate resistance and manipulation. After all, psychologists, counselors, social workers, and other mental health professionals are trained to look for the good in their clients and believe what they say. Therefore, it hurts when the professional discovers that he or she has been the victim of a lie or con. The staff member may have feelings of having a distorted picture of the client (inmate), being duped and betrayed, and being gullible (Gediman and Lieberman, 1996). All of these feelings can produce negative reactions, often strong ones such as rage, toward the inmate-client. It is as though treatment staff consider themselves immune to the lies and cons which inmates perpetrate on everybody else. The authors remind mental health professionals to expect deceit, manipulation, and even personal attacks in their work. Moreover, clinicians should anticipate inmates' noncompliance with treatment plans and difficulty forming a therapeutic alliance with inmates (Gabbard, 2000). Such resistance should be confronted in a manner which is clear, direct, and matter of fact (Decker, 1999).

In addition to personalizing inmates' lies and deceit, treatment staff often overreact when inmates appear not to like them or appreciate their hard work. If a staff member measures his or her competency though perceived liking by an inmate, he or she will be disappointed time and time again. The inmate will sense the employee's need to be liked and exploit this vulnerability in a self-serving manner. Eventually, the staff member will feel devalued and become disillusioned with the entire treatment process (Meloy, 1988). Likewise, it is a big mistake for treatment staff to expect inmates to be appreciative of their time and effort. After all, rarely do inmates enter treatment without some kind of external coercion; they are not, in the purest sense, voluntary clients. Therefore, it should be no surprise that they are unable or unwilling to be grateful for and receptive to the well-intended efforts of staff to help them (Flores, 1997).

Correctional officers, who are conditioned to anticipate and even look for evidence of inmate deception, are by no means immune to conning and manipulation. New officers, in particular, are easy targets for the con and are quite distressed by it (Kauffman, 1988). When they discover that they have been conned, some "rookie" officers take the manipulation so personally that they try to retaliate in some way. This often backfires. For example, one officer learned that he had been conned into letting an inmate leave his cellblock for lunch too early. The officer, who felt that he had been "disrespected," proceeded to delay all of the inmates in that cellblock from going to lunch at the appointed time. The inmates complained to the captain who reprimanded the officer because the lunch schedule was based on housing unit inspections and was not, therefore, subject to variation.

Correctional officers, like treatment staff, must accept the inevitability of manipulation within a correctional population. Officers typically progress through a sequence of naivete followed by extreme cynicism after having been "burned" (Pollock, 1998). Most officers are able to move beyond the cynicism stage and develop a balanced perspective on working with inmates.

Specifically, they do not automatically assume that every inmate is "out to get them," but they are also wise to deception and manipulation. However, even the most experienced and savvy correctional officer still gets conned from time to time. If a particular officer has a reputation of being difficult to fool, then he or she becomes a special challenge for inmates who view themselves as master manipulators. If they are successful at "getting over" on a con-wise officer, they experience a sense of "duping delight" (Ekman, 1992). If the officer takes it personally and overreacts by trying to retaliate every time he or she is conned, then the inmate's duping delight is intensified, especially if other inmates are aware of the manipulation.

Before concluding this section, the reader is reminded that most liars can fool most people most of the time (Ekman, 1992). After all, even young children can successfully deceive their parents. Given the typical inmate's life history of treachery and deceit, not to mention the amount of time he or she has to plan and execute a con, is it any wonder that prison staff find themselves besieged by lies and games? By understanding that manipulation is a product of the inmate's criminal and otherwise distorted thinking style, it is easier to not take such behavior personally. If the employee expends time and energy or vengeance, he or she loses twice: first on the feeling of gullibility, anger, or embarrassment associated with having been conned in the first place, and second, on the resources expended for retaliation (Ford, 1996).

Commandment #7:
Strive for an Attitude of Healthy Skepticism.

As established throughout this book, it is easy to be taken in by a manipulative inmate. On the other hand, it is easy to dislike inmates for what they have done and, in the process, become too cynical, suspicious, and bitter (Ruegg et al., 1997). The authors believe that somewhere on the continuum of "gullibility-cynicism" there exists an optimal perspective for dealing with inmates. Criminal psychologist Stanton Samenow (1984) refers to this outlook as "healthy skepticism." He acknowledges the importance of not being too gullible in working with inmates, but also argues against being so skeptical that the staff member regards everything an inmate does or says as cause for an accusation or interrogation (Yochelson and Samenow, 1977). Otherwise, a correctional officer is likely to become excessively punitive while a counselor or psychologist is apt to become so suspicious that the development of a therapeutic relationship is virtually impossible.

At this juncture, a brief discussion of cynicism and its close relative, hypervigilance, is warranted. Cynicism is the belief that most human behavior is motivated by selfishness (Kirschman, 1977). Cynicism typically results from prolonged exposure to the worst in people's behavior. Correctional personnel certainly see their fair share of that. It takes only a few instances of being conned for an idealistic young staff member to build a self-protective wall of cynicism against being made to look foolish or feel naive. There is so much cynicism in correctional work that the employee easily finds like-minded company to reinforce his or her position.

Hypervigilance is also a potential threat because it is so highly reinforced in the correctional environment. From day one, employees are taught to see everything in the prison environment as suspicious and potentially dangerous. They are trained to develop a habit of scanning the environment for evidence of danger (Kirschman, 1997). As a consequence, some staff are quick to overreact to relatively minor displays of misbehavior or resistance by inmates. Unfortunately, the combination of cynicism and hypervigilance has resulted in excessive uses of force which, in turn, has led to disciplinary action for the offending staff members. Moreover, the authors have noted that some employees tend to carry their suspicion and distrust to their home life, thus creating problems in their primary relationships.

How, then, does one adopt an attitude of skepticism and thereby minimize the personal and professional consequences of cynicism and hypervigilance? One way, according to Sharp (2000), is for staff to be aware of the "zone" within which they are operating in their interactions with offenders. In the "white zone," employees have on their blinders and are largely unaware of what is going on around them. They do not really "see the things a criminal is doing, the criminal's misbehavior or the breaking of rules" (Sharp, 2000, p. 91). Employees operating in the white zone are predictably gullible and overly sympathetic. They tend to accept the inmate's behavior at face value. The staff member is, therefore, especially vulnerable to deception and manipulation.

The opposite of the white zone is the "red zone," in which the correctional employee is so suspicious that he or she is constantly questioning or challenging inmates (Sharp, 2000). Staff members in the red zone are critical, negative, and aggressive. Their relationship with offenders becomes so adversarial that power struggles are inevitable and verbal conflict often ensues. Occasionally, the employee's accusatory and provocative style leads to a physical altercation in which the employee, inmates, or other staff members can be injured. For example, a correctional officer, disliked by inmates and fellow staff alike because of his excessive suspiciousness and verbal abusiveness, provoked a major disturbance in the housing unit for which he was responsible. The officer had accused an inmate of possessing contraband, shouted profanities at the inmate while ordering him to face the wall to be searched, and pushed the inmate into the wall when he responded too slowly. Other inmates crowded into the dayroom and refused to return to their cells. It became necessary for a disturbance control team to use chemical agents to restore order in the unit. A staff member operating in the red zone thus becomes a threat to the safety of staff and inmates and the orderly running of the institution.

Sharp (2000) recommends that employees consistently function in the "yellow zone" in their work with inmates. In the yellow zone, the staff member is neither criticizing everyone nor ignoring obvious or subtle misbehavior. Inmates "are accepted for who they are and unrealistic expectations are not placed on them" (Sharp, 2000, p. 91). The employee is rational, candid, and fair. He or she is neither gullible nor cynical. The authors recognize that staff will occasionally find themselves operating within all three zones. However, if employees strive toward occupying the yellow zone most of the time, they will discover that they do not become burned out, cynical, and angry at the world because their good intentions have been used against them.

Commandment #8:
Do Not Fight the Bureaucracy.

A prison is the epitome of a bureaucracy. It is an organization dominated by rules and paperwork, often ignoring individuals in favor of procedures and precedents (Pollock, 1998). Moreover, correctional institutions adhere to a paramilitary style of management with a vertical chain of command. Obviously, some employees feel more comfortable in and adapt more readily to such an environment than others. Those staff members who struggle with the constraints imposed by the bureaucracy end up either "fighting city hall," which can prove to be exhausting, or succumbing to organizational pressure to conform, which can lead to burnout (Pollock, 1998). The authors contend that it is possible for correctional staff to find a comfortable and professionally satisfying niche within a seemingly rigid and confining environment. To do so, however, requires the acceptance of certain realities about the prison culture, and the adoption of more flexible approaches to meeting one's need for power and control.

Correctional employees are taught how to spot and deal with danger as though it happens every day but rarely, if ever, are they taught to anticipate and manage the daily grind of a bureaucratic system (Kirschman, 1997). Accordingly, organizational stressors, such as rotating shifts and multiple supervisors, affect staff more adversely than the threat of danger from inmates. Correctional workers expect inmates to try to escape and engage in physical violence. They also expect their supervisors and administrators to stand behind them and support their actions when they are accused of doing something wrong. This is especially true when an inmate alleges that a correctional officer has used excessive force or has been otherwise abusive. Unfortunately, the expectation for absolute support from agency administrators is sometimes unrealistic.

Correctional administrators serve many interests and must take the rights and needs of all into account. They are charged with the responsibility for protecting the health and safety of inmates under their care, and insuring that policies and procedures are in place and followed. Moreover, they usually answer to a regional or central office, the legislature and judiciary, and prisoner advocacy groups. A correctional employee, especially if he or she has acted outside the scope of official duties, may not receive the support to which he or she feels entitled. Correctional workers often fail to realize that they exercise considerable discretion in their day-to-day tasks. They have a great deal of autonomy in regard to granting or denying inmate requests, or deciding whether an inmate's cell or person is to be searched for contraband. As long as he or she is operating within the framework of institutional or agency policy and procedures, the staff member's decisions will seldom be questioned or overruled. Indeed, in most cases, there is very little oversight of front line decisions and actions (Schellenberg, 2000). The authors encourage staff to recognize that they have much more authority and influence than they may realize.

Unfortunately, some new employees overlook the "power" they already have and recklessly encroach on other staff members' "territory" in an attempt to "run something." Such boundary intrusions result in conflict between staff, permit inmates to engage in staff splitting, and adversely affect staff morale.

There is, of course, a flip side to the issue of territoriality. Some staff members become so protective of their "turf" that they regard any intrusion by other employees or departments as an attempt to seize control. Such defensiveness flies in the face of the teamwork that is required to effectively run a prison. For example, a few years ago a prison physician wrote a scathing memo to the nursing supervisor on discovery that two diet prescriptions had been countersigned by nurses. He harshly chastised the nurses for overextending their authority and threatened to severely censure any nurses who repeated the mistake. Although the physician was technically correct, the inflammatory and abusive tone of his memo "caused reverberations all the way to (Central Office) with . . . the Secretary of Corrections suggesting that (the physician) be fired" (Marks, 2000, p.111). This is a prime example of how overzealous correctional staff can be in their efforts to retain a sense of power and control within a bureaucracy.

Treatment staff often have an especially difficult time operating within a bureaucratic environment. In most cases, treatment programs are secondary to the custody and security priorities inherent in prison management. Indeed, custodial staff often view counseling or self-help programs as inconveniences in the prison routine. Treatment staff typically find that the prison routine takes precedence over any program-related priorities or agenda (Pollock, 1998). For example, it is very difficult for inmates to be excused from work assignments to attend group counseling sessions. Commonly, an inmate is placed in administrative detention pending some type of investigation, thereby precluding his or her ability to complete a treatment program. Therefore, many mental health professionals find their efforts frustrated by the often insurmountable problems in changing institutional and bureaucratic routines (Boothby and Clements, 2000).

For the helping professional to avoid succumbing to the equally undesirable consequences of "taking on the system"or giving up and doing nothing, the professional must first resolve the issue of mixed or conflicting goals. He or she must show allegiance to public safety (in other words, custody and security issues) and be committed to the individual treatment needs of offenders (Pollock, 1998). Moreover, treatment staff must not personalize the indifference or disdain exhibited in their programs by correctional officers or other nontreatment personnel. The professional also needs to become well acquainted and establish credibility with custodial staff. The first author recalls advice he received from his first boss twenty-seven years ago: "Make friends with the custody staff; they are the backbone of the institution and they'll either make you or break you!" This is easier said than done and requires that treatment staff prove that they support custodial goals and will "be there" if a correctional officer needs assistance. Finally, clinicians need to identify the "key players" in every department. There are the individuals— not necessarily managers or supervisors—who "know how to get things done" within the institution.

Establishing a good working relationship with such persons can make the difference between having an inmate sent to the counseling complex or delaying a group session because the counselor has to walk to a housing unit or work site to collect an inmate. It is useful for mental health professionals to accept the fact that crisis management characterizes the approach of many administrators to running prisons (Pollock, 1998). The safe containment of inmates and the management of their risk for violence takes precedence over therapeutic and programmatic initiatives. In fact, psychiatrists, psychologists, counselors, and the like often have a peripheral role in the overall operation of a prison (Coid, 1998). It behooves treatment staff to demonstrate how their knowledge and expertise can benefit

171

custody and security objectives. For example, mental health professionals have much to offer in the prevention of suicide, violence, risk assessment, and sex offender relapse prediction. The bottom line is that treatment staff must first accept where they sit within the "big picture," and then demonstrate how they can significantly contribute to the broader mission of the institution.

There is yet another way in which correctional treatment staff can achieve a sense of professional satisfaction within the necessary constraints of the prison environment. In short, they can maximize their creativity and flexibility. For example, some mentally ill or emotionally disturbed inmates are housed in maximum-security institutions because of the nature of their instant offense, criminal history, or length of their sentence. They are unable to cope with the stress and danger inherent in the penitentiary milieu and often become victims of predation and exploitation by other inmates. However, it is rarely feasible to transfer an inmate to a medium-security institution without first obtaining a medium-custody classification (Lovell, Allen, Johnson, and Jemelkia, 2001).

To overcome this bureaucratic obstacle, the authors worked with federal prison administrators to establish a mechanism for transferring carefully selected high-security inmates to a medium-security facility characterized by an abundance of mental health resources. Most of these inmates, whose adjustment to penitentiary life was marginal at best, have responded quite favorably to the more therapeutic milieu found in the medium-security facility. This example represents one way of "working within the system" to circumvent a restriction imposed by the bureaucracy itself.

Commandment #9:
Ask For Help.

The authors have observed a profound sense of isolation among many people working in correctional institutions. Despite receiving extensive training regarding correctional policies and procedures, many new employees feel ill-prepared for the challenges of actually supervising and directing the behavior of inmates. Inmates easily spot their insecurity and uncertainties and are quite willing to "educate" the employee regarding his or her duties and responsibilities. The staff member may be reluctant to approach a more experienced employee because of a fear that he or she will appear naive or foolish. The sense of isolation suffered by new employees is exacerbated by the inability of their families and friends to understand what is happening to the employee inside the prison (Kauffman, 1988).

It is, therefore, essential that new employees waste no time actively seeking guidance and support from fellow staff. This is the employee's best protection against establishing an overly familiar relationship with an inmate and ending up in a compromising and perhaps career-ending predicament. Newly employed correctional workers need to seek information from an experienced staff member regarding the prison community as quickly as possible for their own safety, and to prevent future embarrassment as victims of manipulation (Allen and Bosta, 1981). Moreover, if an employee believes that he or she is or was a victim of a con, it is important to tell another staff member and let the inmate know that the manipulation is out in the open. Such exposure deprives the inmate of the ability to exploit the situation further.

Correctional treatment specialists are encouraged to actively seek guidance, direction, and constructive criticism relative to their clinical work with inmates. Mental health professionals are often blind to their limitations in treating such a difficult population; they tend to be unrealistically optimistic about their clients' responsiveness to treatment (Gunderson, 2000).

This can make it easier for inmates to "get over on the shrinks" (Samenow, 1984), since the treatment specialist may incorrectly regard behavioral impairment as evidence of a change in core values. Accordingly, supervision, whether formal or informal, is essential in helping the clinician develop the critical self-awareness necessary for accurately gauging a client's treatment progress (Goldring, 1997). Other ways in which the professional can learn to better deal with inmates include soliciting advice or feedback from more experienced mentors, making use of consultations with colleagues, and establishing peer support groups (Cullari, 1996).

A special problem sometimes exists for female employees working in an all-male prison. They are often perceived as outsiders and subordinates by male employees and, unfortunately, do not always receive the support and mentoring that is so crucial in the correctional environment. In the absence of such support, they must choose to either adapt to the masculine culture, thereby stifling their femininity, and develop a "macho persona" (Arrigo, 2000). This behavior can lead to a negative self-image and lose self-esteem which can, in time, adversely effect their health and family life. It is very important to encourage new female employees to observe and communicate with those women in the institution who have not only "survived" the experience of working in a male-dominated facility, but who have also earned the respect of inmates and male staff alike. This can be accomplished through a well-coordinated staff sponsorship or mentoring program or even through an in-house Employee Assistance Program.

Commandment #10:
Do Not Take Your Work Home with You.

It is very difficult for people outside of corrections to truly understand the frustration and sense of futility inherent in supervising or counseling offenders. Therefore, staff members often turn to one another for understanding and support. This strategy is effective only up to a point. Correctional employees frequently construct thick psychological defenses through which they suppress and deny their emotions (Benner, 2000). This can lead to an even greater source of isolation which, in conjunction with cynicism and hypervigilance, can adversely affect one's worldview. Moreover, a lengthy professional association with a hostile and resistant clientele is, in and of itself, detrimental to staff. Prolonged exposure to the deception and manipulation described in this book can easily result in a jaded view of people in general. Assistance in the form of training, supervision, peer support, and employee assistance programs can be helpful in adopting attitudes of detached concern and avoiding burnout (Lea et al., 1999). Unfortunately, this is not enough. The employee needs to cultivate a balanced life of family, friends, and activities outside of work.

The authors have witnessed countless cases in which a correctional worker's life is restricted to his or her work as a correctional officer, counselor, chaplain, or whatever. They tend to develop a kind of tunnel vision whereby they tend to isolate themselves from others and associate only with other employees. This results in a severely limited reality check on the world (Kirschman, 1997). The situation can even be worse for staff members whose spouse or significant other is also employed at the prison, and for those who work large volumes of overtime. These individuals are seldom able to remove themselves from the prison environment and develop a more balanced worldview. Female correctional officers, as noted above, often feel pressure to change their personality to be accepted by male employees. Unfortunately, they find that they cannot leave their "macho" facade at work and go home and talk to their children in a loud, gruff voice.

Some correctional officers who have failed to achieve balance in their lives are at risk for overstepping personal boundaries with their spouses and children. Their preoccupation at work with finding contraband, avoiding manipulation, and appearing "in control" is often carried over to their homelife. For example, an officer may invade a child's privacy by searching his or her belongings, read the youth's mail, or insist that the child divulge his or her every thought or feeling. Such boundary intrusions closely resemble the custodial and investigative procedures used with prisoners. Several employee assistance program interventions employed by the authors have involved family members who reported that their spouse/parent treated them like inmates. For example, one employee was baffled by his daughter's continued drug use because he had placed her on "thirty-minute checks." The staff member was a correctional officer assigned to a special housing unit where inmates are checked every half hour.

Correctional officers are not the only prison workers who are at risk to take their jobs home with them. Treatment staff can become overly sensitive to issues related to violence, sexual predation, and abuse which they may encounter on a daily basis working with chronic offenders. Moreover, the denial and resistance and poor prognosis for change associated with this population can exert a heavy toll on counselors or therapists. They are likely to take their concerns home and become preoccupied with them, which can lead to despair and emotional unavailability in their own lives. As a result, they may isolate themselves from family and friends, lose their sense of humor, and become too serious and self-absorbed (Decker, 1999).

One of the greatest risks when working in corrections is that staff—whether male or female, or correctional officer or counselor—can take both their work and themselves too seriously. Employees can become so inflated, narcissistic, and self-involved that they risk alienation from their families (Kirschman, 1997). How is such self-absorption and preoccupation with the correctional environment to be prevented or at least minimized? Active involvement with family and friends can help the staff member maintain a balanced perspective regarding other people. Not everybody engages in the deception and manipulation described in this book. In addition, regular participation in sports, hobbies, or other activities can provide the opportunity to complete a task and wind up with a tangible product, something correctional work seldom offers. In short, the authors urge the readers to remember that there is more to life than the job. A truly effective correctional employee will pursue a life filled with healthy family relationships, meaningful friendships, and rewarding leisure time activities. The staff member who makes corrections the center of his or her world will eventually succumb to cynicism and burnout.

Prolonged exposure to inmate deception and manipulation, without regular engagement in authentic and emotionally rewarding relationships with others, can result in no other outcome. The authors urge correctional workers to take good care of themselves as well as each other. After all, even if inmates "get over" on a staff member from time to time, the employee can go home at the end of his or her shift.

Chapter 10

Putting It All Together

The authors have presented a systemic way of understanding the manipulative and deceptive behavior that characterizes criminals. Hopefully, through the scenarios and stories depicted in these pages you have gained a greater sense of the common interactions and ploys that are presented to criminal justice workers every day. It is a fine art to be able to listen to the words and feel affect or emotion underlying them.

Understanding Criminal Behavior

Much of the research having to do with people who commit crimes has been generated by social scientists and criminologists who generally look for broad correlates of crime. For example, the demographic variables most often associated with crime or risk for criminal behavior are young age, male sex, and an urban environment. But when we look at the individual level, demographics have less of a relationship with who commits crime and personal characteristics such as one's values; family and peer support; the ability to reason, plan, and learn from experience; the ability to control impulses; and the ability to feel and respond to love, have a far greater relationship to predicting who commits crime.

We are just beginning to understand the relationship of specific brain disorders or abnormalities that result in the person's inability to feel connected to others. We know from the extensive work of Robert Hare (1993) that psychopaths are devoid of empathy for others. They are cold and callous. Their brains *are* different from "normals" and the regions of the brain that seem to regulate the emotions we associate with caring and compassion do not function properly. When we read about heinous crimes and victims being deliberately tortured, we have a difficult time believing that anyone could perpetrate such cruelties on another. The psychopath is able to sadistically victimize because the psychopath's brain does not register the cues being sent to it by the victim. It only seems to register and relish primitive brain sensations of power (Hare, 1993).

We are also just beginning to understand the disorders of the brain, which have to do with "executive cognitive functioning" or with planning, reasoning out the best solution before acting, control of impulses, and learning from our experiences. The parts of the brain that regulate these functions are in the front of the brain, hence they are called the frontal lobes. Individuals who have experienced brain injury to these areas or who were affected by alcohol that their mothers drank during their pregnancy often behave impulsively and do not learn from their experiences. While this type of brain dysfunction does not "cause" someone to become criminal, it does make them vulnerable to getting into trouble in school, which may lead to expulsion, that may lead to engaging in crimes with others (Fishbein, 2000). Once they enter the criminal justice system, they are too often doomed to recycle, unless a diversion program or treatment program exists to address their specific needs.

Although we have understood the mechanisms of schizophrenia, specifically hallucinations, as a brain disorder that affects the individual's ability to perceive reality, we are just beginning to understand the relationship of schizophrenia and criminality. While it is true that too many individuals who have *only* schizophrenia end up in the criminal justice system, we must accept that a person can have brain disorders in more than one area of the brain so can have schizophrenia and be a psychopath. Certainly, we know a person who has schizophrenia also can have criminal attitudes and values (remember Anthony who tricked the staff to transfer him closer to home by showing them a "fake" letter).

Attitudes are learned and are relatively easy to change (relative to changing brain function). When criminal attitudes are the core traits of the person and that person is also mentally ill, psychopathic, or brain damaged, we indeed have a treatment challenge. The good news is that the approaches you have learned in this book will work well with all of these individuals. Limit setting, relabeling, redirection, and all the others described in these chapters are excellent techniques for interacting with offenders with multiple disorders.

One Final Story

As a relative newcomer to working with inmates, the second author remembers a story told to her by an "old timer." Claude had worked for almost twenty years in corrections, mostly with high security inmates and was finishing up his career as a counselor in a low security institution. He has told the author that years earlier when he was a correctional officer in a penitentiary, he was supervising the inmate orderly who was sweeping the floors around the vending machines in the visiting area. The inmate swept up a quarter and said, "Look, Mr. Smith, I found a quarter." Possession of coins by inmates was prohibited at the facility, so Claude said, "Well, Johnny, I have a nickel here in my pocket. Let's put it with that quarter you found and get you a candy bar out of this machine." Johnny smiled as he ate the candy bar and thanked Claude.

A few weeks later, there was an escape attempt and Johnny was one of the five inmates who had overpowered staff, taken keys, and were set to make their way out of the penitentiary. Claude was one of the staff on duty. The leader of the escaping group gave the order for the others to go back to the officers they had tied up and beat them until they were unconscious! The four inmates headed back to the various rooms where they had put the staff. Johnny headed straight for Claude whose hands were tied behind his back. "Mr. Smith, I'm supposed to beat you and knock you out! I don't want to hurt you—so let's just make this look good." Johnny raised the steel rod he was using as a weapon above Claude's head and brought it down right next to him—missing his head completely. Claude faked a groan and slumped over. Johnny left him and hurried back to the group who made their way out of the unit, although they were later caught.

At the end of the story, Claude looked at me and said, "Funny, isn't it...how a nickel probably saved my life." But, I knew what Claude was really saying. It was not the nickel, it was a simple act of decency that made the difference. Claude, in his way, was advising the author that it is just a good idea to always recognize the humanness in all individuals, no matter their legal status. This is a very simple but important rule of thumb.

You Make the Difference

Much has been written in recent years about successful programs and services for offenders. Anyone who has worked in correctional facilities knows that it is the people who work to deliver services and programs to offenders that really make things happen. Like teachers and textbooks, the greatest textbook cannot compensate for a poor teacher, but a great teacher can compensate for an inadequate textbook. The "teacher" models enthusiasm, reinforces appropriate social behavior, and helps the student on the path of lifelong learning. In many ways, correctional workers are like teachers—encouraging positive behavior, setting appropriate limits, and helping to guide the offender to enjoy a long prosocial life.

Law enforcement personnel and the various individuals in positions in the criminal justice field are "professionals." As with any profession, specific education and training is fundamental and on-the-job experience helps us grow in wisdom and eventually gain mastery in all areas of our field. Each interaction with an offender is an opportunity to learn what works and what does not work. There is no short cut to mastery. We gain experience over time as we engage in our work and reflect on each day as it passes. Because offenders are so different from nonoffenders, there is not much that we know from the free world that works inside a jail or prison. Learning to work effectively with offenders takes time. Be patient. You will make mistakes, get embarrassed, and even feel frightened. But, we guarantee, you will also come to know many everyday heroes and heroines, enjoy the camaraderie of working hand in hand with good, honest people toward a common goal, and feel satisfaction from your work.

We hope this book helps you along your own path to success!

References

AIDS Counseling and Education Program (ACE).1999. *Breaking the Walls of Silence*. Woodstock, New York: Overlook Press.

Albrecht, S. 1997. *Fear and Violence on the Job*. Durham, North Carolina: Carolina Academic Press.

Allen, B. and D. Bosta. 1981. *Games Criminals Play: How You Can Profit by Knowing Them*. Sacramento, California: Rae John Publishers.

Andrews, D. A. and J. Bonta. 1998. *The Psychology of Criminal Conduct, 2nd ed.* Cincinnati, Ohio: Anderson.

Anderews, D. 1995. "The Psychology of Criminal Conduct and Effective Treatment." In J. McGuire, ed. *What Works: Reducing Reoofending–Guidelines from Research and Practice*. New York: John Wiley and Sons.

Arrigo, B. A. 2000. *Introduction to Forensic Psychology*. San Diego: Academic Press.

Benda, B. B., R. L. Corwyn, and N. J. Toombs. 2001. From Adolescent "Serious Offender" to Adult Felon: A Predictive Study of Offense Progression. *Journal of Offender Rehabilitation*. 3: 79-108.

Benner, A. K. 2000. Cop Docs. *Psychology Today*. 33: 36-38, 76.

Bennett-Goleman, T. 2001. *Emotional Alchemy*. New York: Harmony Books.

Berne, E. 1961. *Transactional Analysis*. New York: Ballantine Books.

———. 1964. *Games People Play*. New York: Ballantine Books.

Black, D. W. 1999. *Bad Boys, Bad Men: Confronting Antisocial Personality Disorder*. New York: Oxford University Press.

Boothby, J. L. and C. B. Clements. 2000. A National Survey of Correctional Psychologists. *Criminal Justice and Behavior*. 27: 716-732.

Bursten, B. 1972. *The Manipulative Personality. Archives of General Personality*. 26: 318-321.

Coid, J. M. 1998. The Management of Dangerous Psychopaths in Prison. In T. Millon, E. Simonson, M. Birket-Smith, and R. D. Davis, eds. *Psychopathy: Antisocial, Criminal, and Violent Behavior.* New York: Guilford Press.

Correia, K. M. 2000. Suicide Assessment in Jail: A Proposed Protocol. *Criminal Justice and Behavior.* 27: 581-599.

Cox, M. 1998. A Group-analytic Approach to Psychopaths. In T. Millon, E. Simonson, M. Birket-Smith, and R. D. Davis, eds. *Psychopathy: Antisocial, Criminal, and Violent Behavior.* New York: Guilford Press.

Cullari, S. 1996. *Treatment Resistance.* Boston: Allyn and Bacon.

DeBecker, G. 1997. *The Gift of Fear.* Boston: Little, Brown, and Co.

———. 1999. *Protecting the Gift.* New York: Dial Press.

Decker, D. J. 1999. *Stopping Violence: A Group Model to Change Men's Abusive Behavior.* New York: Haworth Press.

Dutton, D. C. 1995. *The Batterer: A Psychological Profile.* New York: Basic Books.

Ekman, P. 1992. *Telling Lies.* New York: W. W. Norton.

Elliott, B. 1984, October. *Individualized Treatment Within a Peer Group Treatment Program.* Paper presented at the meeting of the Midwestern Criminal Justice Association, Chicago.

Elliott, W. N., M. E. Fakouri, and J. L. Hafner. 1993. Early Recollection of Criminal Offenders. *Journal of Individual Psychology.* 49: 68-75.

Elliott, W. N. and G. D. Walters. 1991. Coping with Offender Resistance to Presentations on the Criminal Lifestyle. *Journal of Correctional Education.* 42: 172-177.

———. 1997. Psychoeducational Interventions with Drug Abusing Clients: The Lifestyle Model. *Journal of Drug Education.* 27: 307-319.

Fautek, P. K. 2001. *Going Straight*. Lincoln, Nebraska: Winters Club Press.

Field, G. 1994. The Effects of Intensive Treatment on Reducing the Criminal Recidivism of Addicted Offenders. In P. C. Kratcoski, ed. *Correctional Counseling and Treatment, 3rd ed.* Prospect Heights, Illinois: Waveland Press.

Firestone, R. W. 1997. *Combating Destructive Thought Processes*. Thousand Oaks, California: Sage.

Fishbein, D. 2000. Introduction. *The Science, Treatment, and Prevention of Antisocial Behaviors: Applications to the Criminal Justice System*. Kingston, New Jersey: Civic Research Institute.

Flores, R. J. 1997. *Group Psychotherapy with Addicted Populations, 2nd ed.* New York: Haworth Press.

Ford, C. V. 1996. *Lies, Lies, Lies: The Psychology of Deceit.* Washington, D.C.: American Psychiatric Press.

Gabbard, G. D. 2000. Combining Medication with Psychotherapy in the Treatment of Personality Disorders. In J. G. Gunderson and G. O. Gabbard, eds. *Psychotherapy for Personality Disorders*. Washington, D.C.: American Psychiatric Press.

Gediman, H. K. and J. S. Lieberman.1996. *The Many Faces of Deceit*. Northvale, New Jersey: Jason Aronson.

Glasser, W. 2000. *Reality Therapy in Action*. New York: Harper Collins.

Gocono, C. B. and J. R. Meloy. 1988. The Relationship Between Cognitive Style and Defensive Processes in the Psychopath. *Criminal Justice and Behavior*. 15: 472-483.

Goldring, J. 1997. *Quick Response Therapy*. Northvale, New Jersey: Jason Aronson.

Gornik, M. 2001. Moving from Correctional Programs to Correctional Practice: Using Proven Practices to Change Criminal Behavior. *Offender Substance Abuse Report*. 1: 60-64.

Gunderson, J. G. 2000. Psychodynamic Psychotherapy for Borderline Personality Disorder. In J. G. Gunderson and G. O. Gabbard, eds. *Psychotherapy for Personality Disorders.* Washington, D.C.: American Psychiatric Press.

Hadley, D. C., J. R. Reddon, and R. D. Reddick. 2001. Age, Gender, and Treatment Attendance among Forensic Psychiatric Patients. *Journal of Offender Rehabilitation.* 32: 55-66.

Hare, R. D. 1993. *Without Conscience: The Disturbing World of the Psychopaths Among Us.* New York: Pocket Books.

———. 1996. Psychopathy: A Clinical Construct Whose Time Has Come. *Criminal Justice and Behavior.* 23: 25-54.

Innes, C. 1997. Patterns of Misconduct in the Federal Prison System. *Criminal Justice and Behavior.* 22: 157-174.

Kauffman, K. 1988. *Prison Officers and Their World.* Cambridge, Massachusetts: Harvard University Press.

Kernberg, O. F. 1998. The Psychotherapeutic Management of Psychopathic, Narcissistic, and Paranoid Transferences. In T. Millon, E. Simonson, M. Birket-Smith, and R. D. Davis, eds. *Psychopathy: Antisocial, Criminal, and Violent Behavior.* New York: Guilford Press.

Kirschman, E. 1997. *I Love a Cop: What Police Families Need to Know.* New York: Guilford Press.

Landay, L. 1998. *Madcaps, Screwballs, Con Women: The Female Trickster in American Culture.* Philadelphia: University of Pennsylvania Press.

Lea, S., J. Auburn, and K. Kibblewhite. 1999. Working with Sex Offenders: The Perceptions and Experiences of Professionals and Paraprofessionals. *International Journal of Offender Therapy and Comparative Criminology.* 43: 103-119.

Lovell, D., D. Allen, C. Johnson, and R. Jemelkia. 2001. Evaluating the Effectiveness of Residential Treatment for Prisoners with Mental Illness. *Criminal Justice and Behavior.* 28: 83-104.

Marek, W. K. 2000. Integrating Cognitive Psychology and Logotherapy for More Effective Treatment. *Correctional Psychologist.* 32: 3-7.

Mark, D. and J. Faude.1997. *Psychotherapy of Cocaine Addiction.* Northvale, New Jersey: Jason Aronson.

Marks, C. 2000. *Behind Barbed Wire.* New York: Vantage Press.

Maultsby, M. 1975. *Help Yourself to Happiness Through Rational Self-counseling.* New York: Institute for Rational Living.

McCann, J. T. 1998. *Malingering and Deception in Adolescents.* Washington, D.C.: American Psychological Association.

Meloy, J. R. 1988. *The Psychopathic Personality: Origins, Dynamics, and Treatment.* Northvale, New Jersey: Jason Aronson.

Meunier, G. F., R. Lett, and K. Ethridge. 1996. Suicidal Behavior among Prison Inmates. *Correctional Psychologist.* 28: 2-6.

Millon, T. and R. D. Davis. 1998. Ten Subtypes of Psychopathy. In T. Millon, E. Simonson, M. Birket-Smith, and R. D. Davis, eds. *Psychopathy: Antisocial, Criminal, and Violent Behavior.* New York: Guilford Press.

Najavits, Lisa M. 2001. *Seeking Safety: A Treatment Manual for PTSD and Substance Abuse.* New York, New York: Guilford Publications.

Oldham, J. M., and L. M. Russakoff. 1987. *Dynamic Therapy in Brief Hospitalization.* Northvale, New Jersey: Jason Aronson.

Padeski, C. A. 1994. Schema Change in Processes of Cognitive Therapy. *Clinical Psychology and Psychotherapy.* 1: 267-278.

Pollock, J. M. 1998. *Counseling Women in Prison.* Thousand Oaks, California: Sage.

Rose, J. D. 1998. *Group Therapy with Troubled Youth: A Cognitive-behavioral Approach*. Thousand Oaks, California: Sage.

Ruegg, R. G., C. Haynes, and A. Frances. 1997. Assessment and Management of Antisocial Personality Disorder. In M. Rosenblath, ed. *Treating Difficult Personality Disorders*. San Francisco: Jossey-Bass.

Salekin, R. T. 2000. Test Review: The Paulus Deception Scale. *American Psychology Law Newsletter*. 20: 3, 8-11.

Samenow, S. E. 1984. *Inside the Criminal Mind*. New York: Times Books.

Schellenberg, K. 2000. Policing the Police: Surveillance and the Predilection for Leniency. *Criminal Justice and Behavior*. 27: 667-687.

Schifter, J. 1999. *Macho Love: Sex Behind Bars in Central America*. New York: Haworth Press.

Sharp, B. D. 2000. *Changing Criminal Thinking: A Treatment Program*. Lanham, Maryland: American Correctional Association.

Sigafoos, S. E. 1994. Conflict Resolution: A Primer for Correctional Workers. In P. C. Kratcocki, ed. *Correctional Counseling and Treatment, 3rd ed.* Prospect Heights, Illinois: Waveland Press.

Simon, R. I. 1996. *Bad Men Do What Good Men Dream*. Washington, D.C.: American Psychiatry Press.

Soderstrom, I. R., T. C. Castellano, and H. R. Figaro. 2001. Measuring "Mature Coping" Skills among Adult and Juvenile Offenders. *Criminal Justice and Behavior*. 28: 300-328.

Stone, M. H. 2000. Good Actions of Antisociality and Responsivity to Psychosocial Therapies. In J. G. Gunderson and G. O. Gabbard, eds. *Psychotherapy for Personality Disorders*. Washington, D.C.: American Psychiatric Press.

Sykes, G. M. and D. Matza. 1970. Techniques of Delinquency. In M. E. Wolfgang, L. Savitz, and N. Johnston, eds. *The Sociology of Crime and Delinquency, 2nd ed.* New York: John Wiley.

Vorrath, H. H. and L. K. Brendtro. 1974. *Positive Peer Culture*. Chicago: Aldine.

Walker, L. E. A. 1994. *Abused Women and Survivor Therapy*. Washington, D.C.: American Psychological Association.

Walters, G. D. 1990. *The Criminal Lifestyle: Patterns of Serious Criminal Conduct*. Newberry Park, California: Sage.

———. 1994. *Escaping the Journey to Nowhere: The Psychology of Alcohol and Other Drug Abuse*. Washington, D.C.: Taylor and Francis.

Walters, G. D. and W. N. Elliott. 1999. Predicting Release and Disciplinary Outcome with the Psychological Inventory of Criminal Thinking Styles: Female Data. *Legal and Criminological Penology*. 4: 15-21.

Walters, G. D. W. N. Elliott, and D. Miscoll. 1998. Use of the Psychological Inventory of Criminal Thinking Styles in a Group of Female Offenders. *Criminal Justice and Behavior*. 25: 125-134.

White, T. W. 1999. *How to Identify Suicidal People*. Philadelphia: Charles Press.

Yochelson, S. and S. E. Samenow. 1976. *The Criminal Personality Vol. I: A Profile for Change*. New York: Jason Aronson.

———. 1977. *The Criminal Personality Vol. II: The Change Process*. New York: Jason Aronson.

Zuckerman, M. 2000. Are You a Risk Taker? *Psychology Today*. 33: 52-56, 84, 87.

Index

S

About the Authors

Bill Elliott received his Ph.D. in counseling psychology from Indiana University in 1985, following the completion of his predoctoral internship with the Federal Bureau of Prisons. He is currently the chief psychologist at the U.S. Penitentiary, Terre Haute, Indiana, where he has been employed since 1984. From 1974 to 1984, he worked as a counselor and administrator at the Rockville Training Center, a correctional facility for juvenile males operated by the Indiana Department of Corrections. In addition, he has served as an adjunct assistant professor with the Criminology Department at Indiana State University since 1980. Dr. Elliott has written articles regarding the management of offender resistance to treatment and regularly conducts training for correctional treatment specialists. He is married and has two grown daughters.

Vicki Verdeyen received her Ed.D. in counseling from West Virginia University in 1978 after completing a predoctoral internship at the Federal Correctional Institution in Morgantown, West Virginia. She served as a drug abuse treatment coordinator at two federal institutions, one for males and one for females, before becoming the first National Employee Assistance Program Coordinator for the Bureau of Prisons in 1988. In 1991, she became the regional psychology administrator for the Mid-Atlantic Region of the bureau and served in that capacity until 1998 when she became the psychology administrator at headquarters in Washington, D.C. In addition to her career with the bureau, Dr. Verdeyen has worked as the supervising psychologist at a juvenile facility for adolescent girls for the State of Virginia. She also served as a psychologist in West Virginia. Dr. Verdeyen has taught undergraduate and graduate courses in criminal justice and psychology for Virginia Commonwealth University and West Virginia University. Dr. Verdeyen has been a licensed psychologist since 1984. She has written articles on the management of violent offenders and changing the criminal mind. Her professional interests are in correctional treatment approaches, the neurobiology of violence, and the integration of psychology practice with the field of corrections.

Learn the Techniques of Conflict Management

Conflict Management and Conflict Resolution in Corrections
Thomas F. Christian, Ph.D.

This resource provides the techniques and tools needed to manage and resolve conflicts in the correctional environment. The author employs a restorative justice approach and stresses the importance of using cooperation and collaboration to resolve any conflict. Basing his information on 35 years of experience in the field, Christian provides practical information for those in facilities, community corrections and mediation. A working vocabulary is included. (1999, 96 pages, 1-56991-096-0)

"Conflict Management and Conflict Resolution in Corrections provides corrections professionals, offenders, victims and other stakeholders a road map for navigating the conflicts of everyday life, and how to collaborate to find a win-win resolution for conflict. The author brings a wealth of experience to the subject as he walks the reader through case studies which identify sources of conflict...this book should be a part of every correctional officer's professional library."

Ron Andring, Sr.
Correctional Lieutenant
Washington State Penitentiary
Walla Walla, Washington

Learn About Mentally Ill Inmate Treatment

Mental Health in Corrections:
An Overview for Correctional Staff

Wesley Sowers, M.D. and Kenneth Thompson, M.D.
with Stephen Mullins, M.D.

Significant mental health issues encountered in jails and prisons today are summarized in this vital resource for correctional personnel. Current treatment options and the involvement of the correctional officer in treatment are the focus of this book. *Mental Health in Corrections* describes inmate behavior and other phenomena related to mental illness and allows the officer to employ four basic steps for dealing with mental health issues: engagement, recognition, assessment of immediate danger, referral to appropriate treatment sources. (1998, 104 pages, index, 1-56991-067-7)

Topics Include:

Substance Abuse Disorders
Problems with Mood
Problems with Thinking
Problems with Fear
Causes of Mental Illness
Biological Treatments

Preventing Mental Illness
Nonmedical Treatments
The Inmates Perspective
Psychotherapy
Rehabilitation
Types of Mental Illness